Grading *and* Learning

Practices That Support Student Achievement

Susan M. Brookhart

Solution Tree | Press

a division of
Solution Tree

555 North Morton Street
Bloomington, IN 47404

800.733.6786 (toll free) / 812.336.7700
FAX: 812.336.7790

email: info@solution-tree.com
solution-tree.com

Printed in the United States of America

15 14 13 12 11   1 2 3 4 5

FSC
Mixed Sources
Product group from well-managed
forests and other controlled sources

Cert no. SW-COC-002283
www.fsc.org
© 1996 Forest Stewardship Council

Library of Congress Cataloging-in-Publication Data

Brookhart, Susan M.
  Grading and learning : practices that support student achievement / Susan M.
  Brookhart.
      p. cm.
  ISBN 978-1-935542-84-1 (perfect bound) -- ISBN 978-1-935542-85-8 (library edition)
  1. Grading and marking (Students) 2. Examinations--Validity. 3. Educational
tests and measurements--United States. 4. Academic achievement--United States--
Testing. I. Title.
  LB3051.B728 2011
  371.27'2--dc22
                                    2011015724

Solution Tree
Jeffrey C. Jones, CEO & President

Solution Tree Press
President: Douglas M. Rife
Publisher: Robert D. Clouse
Vice President of Production: Gretchen Knapp
Managing Production Editor: Caroline Wise
Senior Production Editor: Risë Koben
Text and Cover Designer: Orlando Angel

To Frank, my husband and best friend, for all his love and support

Acknowledgments

Thanks to everyone whose work appears in this book. I would especially like to thank: Leslie Lukin, Lincoln Public Schools; Ric Williams, Everett Public Schools; and Tammy Campbell and Mary Weber, Spokane Public Schools. All of them would hasten to point out that many thanks are due to their colleagues, as well.

Solution Tree Press would like to thank the following reviewers:

Maria Armstrong
Principal
Southwest High School
San Diego, California

Judith A. Arter
Classroom Assessment Consultant
Beavercreek, Oregon

Melanie Hundley
Assistant Professor of the Practice,
   Department of Teaching &
   Learning
Vanderbilt University
Nashville, Tennessee

Nancy Klein Maland
Executive Director of Elementary
   Schools
Knox County Schools
Knoxville, Tennessee

Kent Minor
Lecturer, Department of Social
   Studies & Global Education
The Ohio State University
Columbus, Ohio

Sandranette Sellers
Director, Office of Field Services
Cleveland State University
Cleveland, Ohio

Jody Sherriff
Regional Director, K–12 Alliance—
   Region 2
WestEd
Santa Ana, California

Martha Spriggs
Administrative TOSA
Andersen School
Minneapolis, Minnesota

Table of Contents

Acknowledgments v

About the Author xi

Preface xiii

Chapter 1: All Students Can Learn 3

  The Foundation 3

  How Not to Use Grades 4

  Common Terminology 5

  Student Assessment 7

  External Pressures on Grading Policies 9

  Time for Self-Reflection 10

  Summary 12

Chapter 2: Grading on Standards for Achievement 13

  Why Is It Important to Grade on Standards for Achievement? 15

  Content and Performance Standards 18

  Curriculum Goals and Intended Learning Goals for Classroom Instruction 20

  Building a System for Grading That Supports Learning 22

  Summary 24

Chapter 3: Grading Strategies That Support and Motivate
    Student Effort and Learning 25

  Internal Motivation to Learn 25

  Supporting Students' Motivation 27

  Student Self-Regulation in Action 28

  Student Self-Regulation Through Practice 31

  Exceptions, Exemptions, Differentiation 34

  Twelve Grading Strategies 36

  Summary 38

Chapter 4: Designing and Grading Assessments to Reflect Student Achievement ... 41

Strategy 1: Communicate Clear Learning Targets 41

Strategy 2: Make Sure Assessments Are of High Quality 44

Strategy 3: Use Formative Assessment Before Grading 54

Strategy 4: Inform Students 56

Strategy 5: Grade Achievement, and Handle Behavioral Issues Behaviorally 58

Strategy 6: Grade Individuals 60

Summary 64

Chapter 5: Designing Report Card Grading Policies
to Reflect Student Achievement 65

Standards-Based Report Cards 65

Strategy 7: Grade on Standards 73

Strategy 8: State Grading Policy Clearly 78

Strategy 9: Keep Standards-Based Records 82

Strategy 10: Use Multiple Measures 86

Strategy 11: Maintain Standards-Based Meaning When Blending Evidence 88

Strategy 12: Involve Students 98

Summary 100

Chapter 6: Beginning and Implementing
Learning-Focused Report Card Grading Policies 103

No D, No Zero, and Other Scale-Based Policies 103

Learning-Focused Grading Reforms: Communication Is Key 105

Summary 111

Chapter 7: Communicating With Students and Parents 113

Communicating at the Beginning of the Year 113

Communicating During the Year 113

Communicating at Report Card Time 114

Communicating Beyond the Report Card 115

Summary 125

Chapter 8: Assessing Readiness for Grading Reform 127

Your Individual Practices 127

Your School's or District's Practices 132

Summary 134

Conclusion: Keeping the Promise 135

The Journey to Learning-Focused Grading 137

Unresolved Issues 141

Where Will You Go Next? 141

References 143

Index 147

About the Author

Susan Brookhart, PhD, is a consultant for Brookhart Enterprises, LLC and a senior research associate for the Center for Advancing the Study of Teaching and Learning at Duquesne University. In these positions, Dr. Brookhart contributes her background as a public school teacher and university professor. She is an editorial board member of *Teachers College Record, Applied Measurement in Education,* and *Educational Assessment.* Dr. Brookhart's expertise is in educational assessment, evaluation, and research.

With over 200 publications, presentations, and funded proposals, Dr. Brookhart is a renowned expert on assessment. She has won numerous awards, including the American Educational Research Association Outstanding Paper Award for Special Interest Groups/Classroom Assessment and a Certificate of Research Merit for Special Interest Groups/Classroom Assessment. She has been editor of *Educational Measurement: Issues and Practice* and has also edited several other educational journals throughout her career.

Dr. Brookhart earned a bachelor's degree from Arcadia University. She earned her teaching certificate in Ohio and a doctorate in educational research and evaluation from the Ohio State University.

To book Susan Brookhart for professional development, please contact pd@solution-tree.com.

Preface

The theme of this book is that grading practices should support students in their pursuit of learning. This book brings together my previous research and writing on grading (Brookhart, 1991, 1993, 1994, 1999a, 1999b, 2004, 2009a, 2009b) with stories from my own teaching experience and from other educators with whom I have worked.

My intent is to engage readers who want to reflect on their own or their district's grading policies and practices. Some readers will be teachers who want to experiment with more learning-focused grading practices. Some readers will be administrators who want to support teachers in adopting more learning-focused grading practices. Some readers will be teachers and administrators from districts who have committed to grading reform and are seeking improved methods and practices. Some readers will be teacher education students who are just now contemplating what their philosophy of grading will be. To all these readers, I have one message: It's not about grading. It's about learning.

The point of sending a child to school is for that child to learn, not to get a grade. The point of universal public education is an educated citizenry, not a huge database of grades on millions of students. Grading is just part of the accounting mechanism for learning. This book will, I hope, help your effort to put grading and learning back into perspective and at the same time give you some strategies to make both grading and learning better.

Part 1

THE BASICS OF GRADING FOR LEARNING

Chapter 1

All Students Can Learn

"Will this count for my grade?" an anxious student wants to know. Most students start school wanting to learn, but common educational practices, especially conventional grading, conspire to change students' attitudes as they go through school. By their later elementary school years, most students talk about grades more than they talk about learning, and this preoccupation continues through high school and beyond. As students progress through school, their dissatisfaction with and cynicism about grades increase and their belief in the fairness of grades declines (Evans & Engelberg, 1988). How did it come to this? What have we done?

The Foundation

The premise of this book is the implicit promise or commitment teachers make to their students: *in my class, in this school, all students can learn*. Students won't all learn the same things at the same level of proficiency or in the same amount of time, but if students are in school, they are there to learn *something*. It doesn't take much of a leap to get to the implied questions: So, did they learn? What did they learn, and how well?

Grades are imperfect, shorthand answers to these questions. Assignment grades are summaries of student performance on specific pieces of work. Report card grades are summaries of student performance over sets of work. These sets of work are usually intended to reflect learning goals derived from state or provincial standards. This book will show how to produce grades—both for single assignments and for report cards—that effectively communicate students' achievement of these learning goals.

Of course, grades are not the only answers to these questions. Conferences with students and parents, narrative reports, and other communication methods can supplement grades. Given the number of students in the education system, however, some sort of efficient summary grade has seemed necessary, at least since the advent of the common school (S.G.B., 1840/1992). In almost every school system today, assigning grades is part of a teacher's job. So if you have to do it, you might as well do it well!

Two big ideas follow from this foundation. These ideas should undergird your grading decisions. School and district grading policies should be consistent with them. They are the principles on which all the recommendations in this book are based.

1. Grades should reflect student achievement of intended learning outcomes.

2. Grading policies should support and motivate student effort and learning.

Principle 1 addresses the implicit question "What did students learn (on this assignment or during this reporting period)?" Principle 2 addresses the larger question of how to create the kind of atmosphere that supports learning. Grading policies that are intended to elicit student compliance are not conducive to the active pursuit of learning.

The current climate of standards-based reform forces these issues for us. Perhaps you, too, feel the pressure that other educators have reported from the large-scale student proficiency testing that has been one of the defining features of this reform (Au, 2007). On the face of it, it seems like the pressure of external tests would also ramp up the pressure for traditional scoring and grading practices in the classroom. Paradoxically, though, we can actually use the standards movement to our advantage. Standards describe the objects of students' achievement—what they are to learn—more clearly than conventional grading categories (mathematics, English, music, and so on). This makes room for standards-based grading and other grading reforms that focus on learning and achievement. What matters is not whether the grading practices are standards-based or conventional, but whether they support learning.

How Not to Use Grades

This is a true story about what happens when grades are *not* about learning. I was fresh out of college and had not yet secured my first teaching position. So, like many of you, I did substitute teaching. Within my first month of subbing, I was assigned to cover four days for a high school social studies teacher. Because he knew he was going to be out, he had planned in advance, and we had a brief meeting the week before he left.

One of his classes was composed of ten young men who attended vocational-technical school in the morning and came to the high school in the afternoon for their two required academic classes, English and social studies. According to this teacher, they "didn't want to be there," and he was afraid they would pose a discipline problem while he was gone. Therefore, he had given them a group presentation assignment, and my "lesson plan" was to listen to the groups' presentations, one each day, and grade them. The grades I gave would "stick," he said. By that he meant he would really use them in his report card grades. He hoped that this would motivate the students to behave themselves.

I had just completed an elementary teacher-preparation program and had a brand-new K–8 teaching certificate. I had almost no experience with managing high school students. And what was I given as my only instruction? Grade!

If you think this was a disaster waiting to happen, you're right. When I arrived on Monday, I found that three groups had done absolutely nothing and one student in the fourth group had prepared a few note cards to read to the class. The teacher had asked me to turn in grades to him, so I did. I gave *F*s to the groups that did nothing and a *B* to the group that did something, even though it was pretty dismal. It was clear that the students really didn't care one way or the other.

But the feared discipline problems didn't materialize. The students and I mostly just talked. Back then, I felt I had probably wasted their time, that I should somehow have been able to teach them some social studies. I felt badly that I didn't have enough content knowledge to at least tell them something about their topics. Older and wiser now, I realize that in that context these students weren't really going to learn much anyway.

Why not? There were a lot of reasons, as you can probably tell, but the judgmental use of grades was a big contributor. First, grading in that class was about discipline and control. It was the teacher's "big stick." And in this case, it was to be wielded on ten students who had a long history of being unsuccessful in their academic classes. Not only was this grading plan *not* about learning, but it sent the message to these students that their teacher didn't trust them (and he didn't). Second, I had been instructed to grade the presentations, but there were no criteria for them, no expectations except that they would fill a fifty-minute period and be on certain topics. So the assignment dehumanized the students and disrespected the content at the same time. And group grades are a whole other issue in themselves—see chapter 4 for more about that.

Every time I think of this story, it makes me sad. But I am no longer powerless to do anything about it, as I was then. The grading principles and practices I share in this book are, basically, the opposite of everything in this story. They are designed to help readers be the antithesis of the teacher in this story. Ultimately, they are designed to make school learning better for those ten young men and other students like them.

Common Terminology

Before getting into specifics, it will be helpful to establish definitions for some common terms that will appear throughout this book.

Grade (or *mark*) is commonly used to mean both the mark on an individual assignment and the symbol (letter or number) or sometimes level (such as "proficient") on a report card (Taylor & Nolen, 2005). O'Connor (2009) uses *grade* to mean only the mark on a report card, and not the one on individual assignments. However, the dual usage is so common that perhaps the best way to handle it is to accept it and live with it. That is the approach I will take in this book. I endeavor to be very clear about whether I am talking about individual assignment grades or report card grades.

Grades for individual assignments should reflect the achievement demonstrated in the work. Grades for report cards should reflect the achievement demonstrated in the body of work for that report period. I'll have a lot more to say about that throughout the book, but for now, just consider achievement part of the definition of *grade*.

Scores are numbers. Some individual assignments, most notably tests, receive scores that result from a *scoring* procedure. The scoring procedure should be defined. For example, on a test made up of multiple-choice, true/false, or matching items, a typical scoring procedure is to give one point for each correct answer. Tests that have multi-point problems or essay questions require clear scoring schemes that define how to allocate the points.

Validity means the degree to which grades or scores actually mean what you intend them to mean. In the case of grading, if you intend a report card grade to indicate achievement of a standard, the grade should do that—and not, for example, represent attendance, or how appealing a student's personality is, or something extraneous like that. In the case of a classroom unit test score, if you intend the test score to indicate the achievement of a science unit's learning goals, the score should do that—and not, for example, represent how beautiful the student's handwriting is, or how well the student could read very complicated passages in some of the questions.

Reliability is the level of confidence you have in the consistency or accuracy of a measure. So, for example, in the case of that test score, how close is the percentage correct to the real level of achievement "inside the kid's head," and how much is it influenced by the form of the questions, time of day, inaccuracies in the teacher's use of scoring procedures, and so on? There will always be some inconsistencies (errors) in measurement, but you want to keep them as small as possible.

Grading is only one kind of student assessment or evaluation. Both of these terms, *assessment* and *evaluation*, are broader in scope than grading. *Evaluation* means judgment or appraisal of the value or worth of something. All evaluative judgments, not just grades, should be based on high-quality evidence that is relevant to the particular kind of judgment you are making. *Assessment* is a general term that means any process for obtaining information.

Classes, schools, programs, textbooks, and materials are also commonly evaluated. In this book, we follow the convention that if we are talking about appraisals of students, we will use the term *assessment*. If we are talking about appraisals of classes, schools, programs, textbooks, and materials, we will use the term *evaluation*.

Formative assessment means that students and teachers gather and use information about student progress toward the achievement of learning goals as the learning is taking place. Information from formative assessments helps both students and teachers with decisions and actions that improve learning. *Summative assessment* is assessment that is conducted after the learning has taken place to certify what has been learned. Grading is one form of summative assessment. Unlike formative assessment, in which students must participate, summative assessment is usually the teacher's responsibility.

Student Assessment

Assessment information that is used for grading is only a subset of all the possible assessment information that is available for a student. Assessment information may be about student achievement, but it may also be about students' attitudes, effort, interests, preferences, attendance, behavior, and so on. All of this information is relevant for knowing your students, providing appropriate instruction, taking appropriate action with regard to student behavior, coaching students in their work, talking with them, and inspiring them. So when in this book we say that grades should be based on achievement information only, that does *not* imply that you should ignore the rest of the information you have about students.

Figure 1.1 presents a diagram of the relationships among all the different kinds of information a teacher gathers about students. Discussions of grading often refer to three of these categories: (1) assessment information (everything a teacher assesses about a student), (2) reporting information (only those measures and observations the teacher reports), and (3) grading information (only those measures and observations the teacher reports in a grade representing student achievement) (Frisbie & Waltman, 1992; O'Connor, 2009). Figure 1.1 completes the picture by adding the classroom-only information that the teacher uses formatively and does not report.

Assessment Information
(everything you assess, formally or informally, about students)

Everything—from name and address to health and family to achievement and behavior to attitudes, talents, and dreams—that might possibly be relevant for you to know about students in your class

Information for Feedback
(from formative assessment)

Information for classroom use, with students, or for conferences with students and parents

- About achievement, for furthering learning
- About behaviors and work habits, for coaching effort and studying

Reporting Information
(from summative assessment)

Learning Skills Information

Information from observations of student behaviors that promote learning, like effort and work habits, used to communicate student participation in the learning process, separate from academic achievement, on a report card

Grading Information

Information from summative classroom assessments, used to communicate student achievement of intended learning goals, usually against standards for that achievement

Growth and Progress Information

Information about change in achievement of learning goals (or within subject areas) over time, used to communicate progress on some report cards

Figure 1.1: Venn diagram of relationships among assessment, grading, and reporting information.

External Pressures on Grading Policies

Changing grading policies and practices is not simply a matter of deciding to do something different. Grading happens in a context. This context is somewhat different in each community but often includes pressures from parents and community members and from higher education. These pressures tend to favor conventional, competitive grading practices that rank students. Changing grading policies and practices will require addressing these pressures.

Parent and Community Pressures

Parents and community members have definite expectations for grading policies and practices. However, some of these expectations may not be helpful and may present an opportunity for parent education. For example, even parents of young children seem to want schools to use letter grades and to provide information that compares their child to other students (Huntsinger & Jose, 2009). Yet normative grading—comparing students to one another—is harmful educationally (Ames & Archer, 1988; Dweck, 2000). Moreover, the information that Hannah does something better than Johnny and worse than Yolanda reveals nothing about what Hannah actually knows and can do.

In schools with traditional letter grading, parents sometimes misconstrue the meaning of the letters. The "average" letter grade that most teachers give is a *B*. However, most parents think the "average" grade is a *C* (Waltman & Frisbie, 1994). So parents whose children bring home *C*s may think their student is average when, in fact, the student's grades are among the lowest in the class.

Parents' ideas about grading can vary among different communities. In one study, Chinese American and European American parents of students in grades K–4 had different expectations. The Chinese American parents were, on average, less satisfied than the European American parents with the descriptive scales often used with younger children, such as "1 = consistently demonstrating, 2 = progressing, and 3 = requires additional attention" (Huntsinger & Jose, 2009, p. 404). Both groups wanted comparative information about their children. We know, however, that information about what individual students have actually accomplished is more helpful for teaching and learning.

The larger point here is that you should not assume that everyone shares one perspective on grades and their meaning. You can expect a diversity of perspectives, and you can expect that whatever the perspective, the person holding it thinks it is in the student's best interests. This book will make recommendations for how to communicate your grading policies to parents and how to give them different kinds of information without confounding the meaning of your grades.

Higher Education Pressures

At least at the high school level, teachers and principals perceive expectations for using grading practices that function well to rank students. College and university admissions directors prefer that high schools use grade-point averages based on weighted grades (Talley & Mohr, 1993). In workshop settings, I have often heard high school teachers state that they must give certain kinds of grades because colleges expect it. I have even heard middle school teachers say that they must give certain kinds of grades because parents want to be sure their children will be ready to gain admission to selective colleges and universities.

To be honest, I think some of those teachers were copping out. ("I don't want to change my grading practices, and here's an excuse not to.") But some of them were expressing a real dilemma and real discomfort at confrontations with assertive parents. Some districts address this dilemma by using standards-based report cards in elementary and sometimes middle school; then in high school they use standards-based grading practices with either traditional report cards or adapted versions of standards-based report cards that still yield grade-point averages.

Time for Self-Reflection

Take a moment to think about your own approach to grading, your own history with it, and in general where you're coming from when it comes to grades and grading. Everyone's grading background is a little different. In fact, my own grading background is part of what led me to write this book. So first, I ask that you give serious reflection time to the questions in figure 1.2.

Reflect on your personal experience with grading.

1. Do you have a story from your own career as a student where grades play a prominent role? If so, tell that story. What did you learn from it?

2. When you first became a teacher, did you feel prepared to "give grades" to students, either on individual assignments or on report cards? Describe your first efforts at grading and what you learned from them.

3. What are the main principles you use in your current grading practices? How have they been influenced by your previous experiences?

4. Are you satisfied with your current grading practices? Where do you want to focus your next steps in the development of your grading practices?

Figure 1.2: Self-reflection questions on your grading background.

Now that you have answered these questions, I will share my personal reflections (figure 1.3). How is your story like mine? How is it different?

1. Do you have a story from your own career as a student where grades play a prominent role? If so, tell that story. What did you learn from it?

    As high school juniors, a girlfriend and I were tied in class rank. Senior year, she took a more difficult schedule than I did, and she learned more. But she got a B in a college-level biology course, so she slipped behind me in class rank. At the end of senior year, I got an academic prize that was based on class rank. I felt like a fraud. My senior year "coasting" had resulted in grades that made me look smarter than my friend, and it wasn't true. At the time, I just felt bad. With hindsight, I believe that was a pathetic lesson to have taught two excellent students.

2. When you first became a teacher, did you feel prepared to "give grades" to students, either on individual assignments or on report cards? Describe your first efforts at grading and what you learned from them.

    My teaching career began with a half year of daily substituting. Then I accepted a position in a third-grade classroom when the teacher left at the December break. Three reading groups were already in place, and the gradebook was already set up, including places for "oral read-ing" grades. So there I sat, with a group of seven students taking turns reading out loud to me while the rest of the class was doing seatwork. I had no criteria, no grading scale (what should I put? A? 100? 4?), and no experience with grading oral reading. Each reading group, and each student in each group, read something different. I just "made it up." I put 100 for readers whose work I liked, and 90, 80, and 70 for lesser performances, although I could not have told you in any given case why I came up with the scores I did. Again, I felt like a fraud.

3. What are the main principles you use in your current grading practices? How have they been influenced by your previous experiences?

    Influenced by the experiences I have already recounted and others like them, I read research on grading and did some research on the subject myself. I have become thoroughly convinced that no grading system will ever be perfect but that, on balance, grading on achievement is the best policy. It solves many grading problems, and it is defensible education-ally. Grading on achievement gives students information about what they know and can do, and it supports students' self-regulation and feelings of control over their learning.

Figure 1.3: The author's personal reflections on grading.   continued →

4. Are you satisfied with your current grading practices? Where do you want to focus your next steps in the development of your grading practices?

    I feel like I have arrived at the right principles (grading on achievement and grading to motivate learning). Like most people, I always need practice at making this happen for every student, all the time.

Summary

The big ideas in this chapter are that grades should be based on achievement and that grades should support student motivation and learning. These two big ideas form the foundation for the rest of this book and all the principles and examples in it. This chapter began with a bad example of a class in which these principles were *not* followed. I hope the story illustrated the big ideas "in the breach." The chapter then reviewed some terminology and briefly discussed some external pressures that affect the context of grading, Finally, I hope the reflection you just did helped you identify any internal grading pressures that exist for you. With all this as preparation, chapter 2 presents a more systematic statement of the rationale for learning-focused grading, beyond the stories and anecdotes in this chapter. There is quite a bit of evidence to support these big ideas about grading, learning, and motivation.

Chapter 2

Grading on Standards for Achievement

Grading on standards for achievement means a shift from thinking that grades are what students *earn* to thinking that grades show what students *learn*. Teachers sometimes talk about grades as pay students earn by doing their work. This seems fine as a simple image. After all, doing assignments, studying, and paying attention are the work students do when they're in school. But if "earning" grades gives people the idea that grades are students' pay for punching a clock, for showing up and being busy, and for following directions no matter what the outcome, then the image is harmful. The object of all this busy-ness isn't just the doing of it. The idea is that once students do all these things, they will learn something.

One time when I was conducting a district workshop on grading, a young teacher became agitated. Everything her students did "counted," she said. Everything! That was what they were in school for, and that was how she kept them in line. If behavior and work habits didn't count toward grades, her classroom would fall apart. It would be easy to mock this teacher, but maybe we can learn something valuable from her. I think she really believed what she was saying and genuinely could not imagine coping with her classroom, much less being "successful" (according to her own judgment), without the heavy-handed grading policy she described. In fact, her resistance to my ideas might have been rooted in a fear that she really wasn't a good teacher yet, and she might have realized deep down that being an "enforcer" wasn't a very educative teaching style.

For grading to support learning, grades should reflect student achievement of intended learning outcomes. In schools today, these learning outcomes are usually stated as standards for achievement. Grades on *both* individual assessments and report cards should reflect students' achievement of performance standards on intended learning outcomes. It has to be both, because if grades on individual assessments don't reflect achievement of intended learning outcomes, the report card grade derived from them can't, either. The report card grade is a summary of the meaning of a set of individual grades.

Before we go any further down this road, stop a minute and reflect on what you think about this principle. Probably most of you reading this book do not have quite as extreme a view about "grading everything" as my agitated teacher did. However, many of you may genuinely think students should be graded for practice work, effort, and perhaps even attitude and can explain why you think so. While I do not hold this view, I acknowledge that if behavior, effort, and attitude are not included in the grade, they have to be assessed and handled in some other way.

Please take a moment to ask yourself the reflection questions in figure 2.1.

Reflect on your current grading beliefs and practices. If you teach more than one grade or subject, think about them one at a time as you contemplate these questions. For each question, try to figure out the rationale behind your answer. Why do you think or grade in the manner you describe for each question?

For individual assignment grades:

1. What symbol(s) do you use for grades (A,B,C,D,F, rubric levels, percents, other)?

2. What meaning do you intend those symbols to carry (achievement, effort, improvement, comparison to other students' work, other)?

3. How do you grade if work is late? Sloppy? Missing?

4. What do you do if the work falls on the borderline between two grade categories?

For report card (summary) grades:

1. What symbol(s) do you use for grades (A,B,C,D,F, performance standard levels, percents, other)?

2. What meaning do you intend those symbols to carry (achievement, effort, improvement, comparison to other students' levels, other?)

3. What elements do you include in your report card grades, and in what proportions (tests, quizzes, projects, papers, homework, effort, ability, participation, improvement, attitude, behavior, other)?

4. What method do you use to combine these assessments into a summary grade for the report card?

5. What do you do if the student's summary grade falls on the borderline between two grade categories?

Figure 2.1: Self-reflection questions on your current grading practices.

Why Is It Important to Grade on Standards for Achievement?

Ms. Davis was a teacher in a self-contained fourth-grade classroom. Like many other teachers in her building, Ms. Davis believed students earned their grades by doing their work, which included things like showing a good attitude toward school, participating in classroom life, and trying hard. Courtney and her friend Aaliyah loved Ms. Davis's class. They enjoyed the family feeling, and they would do anything Ms. Davis asked.

This enthusiastic participation extended to their academic work as well. Courtney and Aaliyah always completed their work when asked, tried hard, and behaved well during lessons. They raised their hands and spoke during class discussions. The quality of their work and their understanding in reading and language arts were good, but in mathematics—not so much. However, because they were such sweet students, their report cards carried A grades for all three subjects. In mathematics, Ms. Davis made sure there were ways for Courtney and Aaliyah to earn extra points. For example, they could do simple bonus questions or help with the mathematics bulletin board.

Courtney's and Aaliyah's parents saw these As and thought the grades meant that their daughters understood their mathematics as well as they did their reading and language arts. Sadly, so did Courtney and Aaliyah. They didn't realize they had been "cut a break." They thought they were doing and learning what was important to do and learn in mathematics. Imagine everyone's surprise when the state test results indicated they were both "below basic" in mathematics at the end of fourth grade. Imagine the special disappointment of the two little girls, who really thought they were learning. They had trusted their teacher to teach them and had interpreted their As as evidence that they had learned. Along the way, they had missed many learning opportunities because they thought all was well. Instead of earning bonus points, Courtney and Aaliyah could have been practicing specific concepts and skills. But they didn't know.

Unfortunately, stories like this are all too common. If such missed learning opportunities continue for several years, students end up far enough behind that they cannot recover (Sanders, 1998).

Research Support

The recommendation to grade on standards of achievement only, separating assessment of effort, improvement, and behavior into a separate appraisal, is the current mainstream recommendation. It is not the mainstream *practice* yet, because it takes a lot of time to change practice. In fact, that is part of the reason I wrote this book—to help people who would like to move to grading on standards of achievement. Many grading authors recommend achievement-based grading (Guskey & Bailey, 2001; Marzano, 2010; O'Connor, 2009, 2011; Scriffiny, 2008; Wiggins & McTighe, 2006; Winger, 2005, 2009), as have I in my previous writing on the subject (Brookhart, 2004, 2009a). Achievement-based grading follows logically and reasonably from what we know about successful teaching and learning.

Achievement-based grading brings up an interesting question. If a district claims that curriculum and instruction are aligned with state standards and the district uses a standards-based grading system, it makes sense that students' proficiency according to teacher-assigned report card grades should be related to their proficiency according to state test results. Is it?

There is evidence that traditional grades and state test results are only moderately related (Brennan, Kim, Wenz-Gross, & Siperstein, 2001; Conley, 2000). The inclusion of nonachievement factors in grades is usually offered as the reason for this lack of congruence between grades and external measures of achievement (Brennan et al., 2001), and there is research evidence to support that reasoning (Brookhart, 1993, 1994; Willingham, Pollack, & Lewis, 2002).

D'Agostino and Welsh (2007; Welsh & D'Agostino, 2009) investigated the question of whether achievement-only, standards-based grading yields accurate information about students in terms of their performance on state tests. What they found lends strong support to the use of a range of recommended grading practices, but most especially (a) being performance focused, defined as measuring standards of achievement rather than effort, and (b) assessing the full range of the performance objectives under a standard, not just some of them.

In the district they studied, D'Agostino and Welsh (2007) found that the overall agreement rate between third- and fifth-graders' standards-based grades and their proficiency levels on the Arizona Instrument to Measure Standards (AIMS, the Arizona state test) were only moderate: 44 percent for mathematics, 53 percent for reading, and 51 percent for writing. When corrected for chance agreement, those percentages fell even lower (16 percent to 26 percent). However, when the researchers looked at these statistics for individual classrooms, they found wide variation. In some classrooms, the convergence between graded and tested standards-based performance was much greater than in others.

To see whether grading practices were related to how well teachers' judgments matched student proficiency levels, the researchers coded information from interviews of each teacher according to whether the following recommended grading practices were "clearly evident," "somewhat evident," or "not evident" (Welsh & D'Agostino, 2009, p. 85):

- Assessing most of the performance objectives in state standards

- Grading on achievement, not effort

- Creating or obtaining assessments focused on state standards

- Identifying the objectives assessed by each assessment and tracking students' performance skill by skill

- Focusing on attainment of standards, not objectives listed in textbooks

- Using end-of-unit assessments for grading, not practice work

- Focusing on achievement, not progress (improvement)

- Assessing frequently

- Using multiple assessment approaches to measure different aspects of a skill

- Using a clear method for converting individual assessment results to standards-based grades

Interestingly, they found that this list of attributes scaled nicely into an "appraisal style" score and that the two heaviest contributors to the score were, as mentioned, basing grades on achievement (performance quality) rather than effort and assessing the full range of objectives (knowledge and skills) in each standard. And even more interesting, the higher the appraisal-style score—that is, the more a teacher's grading practices followed these recommendations—the more closely that teacher's grades agreed with his or her students' tested proficiency levels.

This study is the only one I know of that has tried to answer the question of whether grading practices make a difference in the quality of information on standards-based report cards. It was based on two years of data for two grades in one district in Arizona, and I hope soon to see other studies of this kind. For now, though, this study helps move the recommended grading practices one step further down the "research-based" road. Grading-practice recommendations—for example, to grade on achievement and not effort—are based in theory and research from the fields of educational psychology and measurement. As such, they are research-based principles. This study gives us a direct test of the application of those principles in practice.

Benefits for Teaching and Learning

It is important to evaluate what we value, and students want to do what counts. Grading on achievement says we value learning. It reinforces the commitment about learning we make to students and parents.

If grades are based on achievement, students and teachers can use the information better than if the grades represent a mixture of learning and other factors. Teachers can use achievement-based grades as indicators of the success of their instruction and as information to help them plan next steps in instruction for individual students, groups of students, or whole classes. Students can use achievement-based grades to self-assess and to set goals. A high school student could, for example, decide to spend more time studying for tests in a certain class. An elementary student might realize she needs help in a certain area and ask for it. These student uses hint at another benefit of grading on achievement: supporting student motivation to learn.

Grading on achievement, with a coherent system of instruction and formative assessment deeply aligned with the criteria for achievement, can lead to students' developing a deeper and more self-regulated sense of responsibility than the use of grades as external rewards and punishments for behaviors. When students understand that it is their achievement against standards that is graded, most of them will respond by developing the self-regulation and study skills necessary to achieve.

Basing grades on achievement doesn't mean we don't care about students' behavior, attendance, ability to meet assignment deadlines, degree of effort, and so on. Of course we do! All of these factors have a direct impact on learning, and it is in this light that we should interpret them to students. Developing good habits in all of these areas will help students be the best learners they can be.

For the most part, handle behavior and "academic enablers" (learning skills such as work habits, effort, taking homework seriously, and so on) by coaching, not reporting. Use informal assessment to monitor these skills day by day. Give students ongoing formative feedback about these behaviors and suggestions for how to adjust them. Ultimately, study skills, classroom citizenship, and other learning-enabling skills can be reported using a separate indicator system on standards-based report cards. But they do not belong in the proficiency scales or in the letter grades that indicate achievement.

I hope that by this point I have demonstrated that grading on achievement is the main principle by which we keep our commitment to students: *in my class, in this school, all students can learn*. We have to make clear to students *what* they are learning and how well. We have to give them grades based on their achievement.

Content and Performance Standards

If we agree to base grades on achievement, the next question is "Achievement of what?" The usual answer in this day and age is achievement of state or provincial standards. In the United States, as of 2011, all fifty states and the

District of Columbia have state standards. Most states organize these into content standards and performance standards. *Content standards* are statements of what students should know and be able to do. Content standards are usually organized by subject (for example, reading, mathematics, science) and by grade level. *Performance standards* are statements about how well students are supposed to know and be able to do what the content standards list.

Performance standards are defined differently in each state. For performance overall, each state defines three, four, or five levels of performance. The names of these levels vary slightly from state to state. For example, the state of Pennsylvania uses four levels: below basic, basic, proficient, and advanced. Each performance level is associated with a cut score on the state test (that is, the minimum score a student must attain to qualify for the level) and *should* also be associated with a performance-level descriptor (that is, a statement of what the level means) (Perie, 2008).

Each state's set of standards is different. Standards differ in grain size (level of detail). Some states' standards are very general; others are very specific. Some states have general standards with more specific "strands" or subdivisions of content and skills under the standards. At the most general level, states' standards are more similar than different, with the exception that in many states, students are expected to understand the history, geography and environment, and economics of their own state.

On June 2, 2010, the National Governors Association Center for Best Practices and the Council of Chief State School Officers released a set of state-led education standards called the Common Core State Standards in English Language Arts and Literacy in History/Social Studies, Science, and Technical Subjects and Common Core State Standards for Mathematics. The text of these standards is available at http://corestandards.org. The intention is that states will adopt these as at least 85 percent of their state standards.

Mid-continent Research for Education and Learning (McREL) publishes *Content Knowledge*, 4th edition, an online compendium of content standards and benchmarks for K–12 education, available at www.mcrel.org/standards-benchmarks. This compendium is organized into standards that transcend grade levels. Under each standard there are grade-level statements of what students in that grade should be able to do, which McREL calls "benchmarks."

The College Board offers the College Board Standards for College Success (http://professionals.collegeboard.com/k-12/standards) in English/language arts, mathematics and statistics, and science. These standards are intended to define the knowledge and skills students need in order to be college- and career-ready. These standards also describe a pathway of knowledge and skills to advanced placement readiness. The College Board's goal is to increase the number and diversity of students who are prepared to enroll in college and to succeed in 21st-century careers.

Professional disciplinary organizations, such as the National Council of Teachers of Mathematics, National Council of Teachers of English, National Council for the Social Studies, National Academy of Sciences, National Science Teachers Association, and Teachers of English to Speakers of Other Languages, are also excellent sources of information about what students should know and be able to do. In fact, the disciplinary organizations were at the forefront of standards development.

For me, the takeaway point from all these standards is that states and national organizations have given thought to organizing and presenting a description of the learning students can be expected to accomplish during their schooling. In some ways, it is a description of the promise: standards describe *what* all students can learn. And while the formulation of standards in your state is the one to which you and your students will be held accountable, the other formulations have good ideas about what that learning means, too. You may get some good ideas by looking at several sets of standards in the content area you teach.

Curriculum Goals and Intended Learning Goals for Classroom Instruction

The "standards" on which you grade achievement for individual assignments and for report cards are not exactly the state or Common Core standards discussed in the previous section. The standards on which you grade students are your actual expectations for their learning for that assignment or that report period. They are usually narrower in scope than state standards, which are typically broad. Expectations for student learning are derived from state standards and then translated or subdivided into curriculum goals and then into intended learning goals for classroom instruction. This is a distinction some people have a hard time making, probably because the word *standards* is used for both state standards and curriculum and classroom learning goals.

A state's annual state test is aligned to the state standards, but that state test is intended to be a general summary of learning over the course of at least a year. Any one standard is usually covered by just a few test items, and the scores reported for accountability purposes are aggregated across all standards to report proficiency levels in subjects (for example, mathematics, reading/ language arts, science). And while one of the points of being "standards-based" is alignment, which means that the same standards are the basis of planning, instruction, assessment, and ultimately achievement, it is important to know that the curricular standards and learning goals for classroom lessons are not state standards per se but derived from them.

It is common to derive classroom unit goals and lesson objectives by reducing the grain size (that is, increasing the specificity) of concepts and skills so they are appropriate for lessons and units of instruction. This should not change the ultimate goals for learning. For training-style objectives (those that involve a very specific performance), state the specific learning outcome, even if you use the same language as the standard. For example, an outcome might be "Adds two-digit whole numbers." This statement is derived from the Common Core mathematics standard 2.NBT.6, "Add up to four two-digit numbers using strategies based on place value and properties of operations" (Common Core State Standards Initiative, 2010b, p. 19).

Most learning outcomes are not that specific, however, and they focus on understanding terms and concepts in such a way that they can be applied both to tasks similar to those in which the concepts were learned and to tasks beyond that. You will hear such learning outcomes described variously as requiring "higher-order thinking skills" or "21st-century skills" or "deep knowledge." For this kind of learning outcome, deriving learning goals for instruction and assessment requires two steps. First, state the general standard clearly; then specify what sorts of performances—among many that you could choose—will be evidence of mastery of that standard (Gronlund & Brookhart, 2009).

For example, a standard might be that students can comprehend literal information from informational text and use it to make inferences: Common Core Standard ELA, Reading Standards for Informational Text K–5, grade 4, #1: "Refer to details and examples in a text when explaining what the text says explicitly and when drawing inferences from the text" (Common Core State Standards Initiative, 2010a, p. 14). How will you know when students can do this? State the general standard first, and then list performances that clarify it. Assess these performances, *but realize they are a sample of all the possible performances students could do to show you they can recount literal information and use it to make inferences.*

Your grades on individual assignments, then, are a sample of scores from a larger, potential, unmeasured set of performances. So you might have something like the following list of performances for the general standard:

1. Students comprehend literal information from informational text and use it to make inferences.

    1.1. Students recount the details from a passage of informational text. [This performance description could be further limited by specifying a grade level and/or specific kind of text—for example, fourth-grade social studies textbook; newspaper article; or cookbook and craft directions.]

1.2. Students summarize information by giving main points and supporting details.

1.3. Students draw conclusions about what interests and skills successful readers of the text might need.

1.4. Students compare and contrast information from this passage with information from other passages they have read.

1.5. Students draw pictures depicting details from the informational text.

1.6. Students explain to other students what they learned from reading the text.

1.7. Students make or do something based on information from the text.

This planning procedure makes clear that the instructional objective is *comprehension* and not *recounting, summarizing, drawing conclusions, comparing and contrasting, drawing, explaining,* or *making something.* This list is simply a *sample of the types of performance that represent comprehension.* A different sample of specific types of performance could serve equally well.

Building a System for Grading That Supports Learning

To build a system for grading that supports learning, all the elements in the system need to work together. The system is bigger than just your grading policies. You must clearly articulate what your learning outcomes are and how well students need to attain them in order to be considered proficient (or to reach an acceptable level of mastery in whatever reporting system you use). You must also be able to say how your classroom learning outcomes map onto both the larger curricular standards that are graded on the report card and the still-larger state standards that are tested annually. Building a system like this is important for instruction and for curricular coherence as well as for grading.

Only after you can describe what you will expect students to know or do can you start defining the assessments that will enable you to find out if they know and can do it. This sounds obvious, but in the heat of practice, teachers often skip this step. They sometimes go for a fun project because it sounds like fun, without first checking to see if it deeply matches the intended learning of content, thinking skills, and other discipline-related skills (for example, writing like a scientist). So it's important to say this: each assessment (or assessed project or assignment) needs definitions for each performance level, and these need to be communicated to students before they begin work. Unless students are *aiming* for something, it's not a target.

Only when standards, instruction, practice and formative assessments, and individual graded (summative) assessments are aligned can you begin to consider your grading system standards-based. No amount of standards-based grading recommendations (clarify performance levels, grade on achievement, and so on) can make a system standards-based if the original evidence of achievement is not soundly standards-based work.

When you are sure the building blocks of the system are in place—that individual pieces of graded work are standards-based—you'll need to use strategies that make the next layer of the system standards-based as well. You'll need a recording method that can keep track of students' performance on individual skills, or at least on the standards as articulated on the report card. You'll need to use methods to combine individual grades to reflect the achievement status a student ultimately reaches on each standard. And of course you'll need reporting methods that allow you to express this information in a clear, meaningful report card (Guskey & Bailey, 2001, 2010).

How Can I Grade on Standards if My School Doesn't Use "Standards-Based" Report Cards?

If standards-based grading is not the reality where you are at the moment, don't despair. You can still do a good job of applying grading principles that support student learning. If you are a teacher in a district with conventional report cards, you can still use the two grading principles that honor the commitment to learning: (1) assign grades that reflect student achievement of intended learning outcomes, and (2) adopt grading policies that support and motivate student effort and learning. You can do this by clearly communicating your "standards" (in the sense of expectations for work quality) to students and grading on that basis.

In a traditional grading context, for example, you might be required to report subject grades (English, mathematics, and so on) with a letter scale (*A*, *B*, *C*, *D*, *F*). Make clear for each assignment what the learning target is and how the assignment will allow students to show that particular knowledge or skill set. Have students look at some examples of good work if possible. Make sure students know what practice opportunities they will have and what formative assessment opportunities you will provide so that they can gauge where they are and how they need to improve before submitting work for grading or taking a test.

Then, even though you will have to summarize assessments of several different standards into one overall subject grade, at least you and the students will know exactly what the grade means, because all of you will be able describe the set of knowledge and skill demonstrations on which it is based. Make sure the proportions you use to combine the different individual assessments into a final grade are the same proportions you used for your instructional emphases and that students know what they are. In doing this, you are taking care of Principle 1—that grades should reflect student achievement of intended learning outcomes—within the traditional grading context.

You can also stay true to Principle 2—that grading policies should support and motivate student effort and learning—within a traditional grading context. The idea of using formative assessment for practice work and not taking a summative grade until students have had an opportunity to learn the knowledge and skills for which you are holding them accountable can be applied directly in your classroom assessments in a traditional grading context. That is the most important and powerful of the strategies that support and motivate student effort and learning. If grades are not what you "give" but what students accomplish, then—as one teacher I know puts it—students "know what they need to do" to get the grades they desire.

Many high schools that want to adopt standards-based grading follow the very approaches just described. They don't change their report cards, or don't change them much (perhaps adding in a work-habits scale for each class), in order to maintain the possibility of conventional grade-point averages for college admissions and other purposes. But they do make sure that the grades reflect achievement, and they adopt grading policies that support student motivation and achievement.

Summary

One big idea in this chapter is that the use of standards-based or, more generally, learning-focused grading is supported by a multitude of evidence and potential benefits. Another is that the standards in state or national documents are often of a larger grain size than the standards for instruction, assessment, and grading. This means that districts and teachers must take steps to ensure that their curriculum, instruction, and grading are all aligned to state standards. The third big idea in this chapter is that even in a traditional grading context, learning-focused grading is not only possible, but recommended.

Chapter 3

Grading Strategies That Support and Motivate Student Effort and Learning

When I was teaching seventh-grade English in a middle school, we gave standardized tests once a year, toward the end of the school year. It took about a week to administer all the subject tests. This was a long time for some students. To make sure students were "motivated" to do their best, the principal declared that any student who received a misbehavior notice during the testing (indicated by having one's name put on the board) would not be eligible to participate in Field Day, which was scheduled for the next week. Since this particular standardized test didn't seem relevant to students' lives in any other way, this was probably a reasonable approach.

This story is a good example of *external* motivation. The authority to allow participation in Field Day was external to the students. Most of them behaved in order to get something from someone else, in this case to get Field Day permission from their teachers and principal. Often in schools, I have heard teachers and principals use the term *motivation* in this external sense. External motivators work best for short-term goals that have only indirect relevance to students' lives.

Internal Motivation to Learn

Another kind of motivation is *internal* motivation. This kind of motivation is better for learning and, ultimately, more important in life in general.

Self-Determination

A fundamental aspect of internal motivation is self-determination. *Self-determination* is a motivator for people of all ages. People would rather do what they have decided to do than what others tell them to do. This goes for little children ("Me do it!"), students, and adults. Self-determination theory says that people need three basic things: a sense of belonging, a sense of competence, and a sense of autonomy (Ryan & Deci, 2000).

Grading practices that support student self-determination give students some feelings of control over their grades. Students need the feeling that their deliberate actions—studying, paying attention, asking for help, and so on—can have an effect on their learning and thus their grades, if they choose. Self-determination and control are basic motivators in all areas of life, not just school.

Self-Regulation

Self-regulation in learning is the ability to monitor one's own learning and select appropriate strategies to use to continue learning (Boekaerts, 1999; Butler & Winne, 1995; Perry, Phillips, & Dowler, 2004). Self-regulation is another important aspect of internal motivation to learn.

Grading practices that support student self-regulation have to afford students some strategies they can use to affect their learning and their grades, if they choose. Students need to feel that their effort, prudently applied, will in fact lead to increased achievement and therefore better grades. And they won't feel that way if it isn't true under the grading policy used in their classroom. For instance, if a student who falls behind can't catch up no matter how much self-regulation he employs, because his average is already ruined, why should he try? In school, self-regulation can be one of the means students use to create for themselves a sense of competence and autonomy, or self-determination.

Self-Efficacy

Yet another important aspect of internal motivation is the frame of mind exemplified by students who have mastery of learning goals. The act of learning and the feeling of "knowing something" is in itself an encouragement (Ames & Archer, 1988). Grading practices support mastery goals when they indicate that students have learned something specific. Grading practices support mastery goals when students can tell you what the grade indicates they have learned and how they directed their efforts in order to learn it.

Building up enough of these experiences in which students feel they know something contributes over time to students' self-efficacy as learners (Bandura, 1997; Pajares, 1996). *Self-efficacy* as a learner is a student's belief that he or she can, in fact, learn effectively. It is usually specific to a subject, and sometimes to tasks or skills within a subject. Students can feel efficacious as math learners but not as readers, for instance. Students who understand how they learn and who control their own learning (self-regulated students) are more likely to feel like effective learners or to exhibit self-efficacy for learning some content.

Supporting Students' Motivation

The important takeaway point about all these "self" qualities is obvious but worth spelling out here. Internal motivation is all about the *student's* beliefs, thoughts, feelings, and actions. It is not about the *teacher*. The teacher is responsible for grading, but it is the students who do the learning. Grading policies and practices can either support students' feelings of self-determination, self-regulation, and self-efficacy, or they can inhibit them. Good grading policies and practices do the former. Consider the following story of a teacher who wanted to help a student develop better self-regulation.

> *Mr. Miller taught seventh-grade social studies in a middle school. Jayden was one of his most able students, but he had a mischievous streak and seemed to enjoy the notoriety that came with his "outlaw" status. In the past, Jayden's misbehavior had often affected his grades. Mr. Miller believed that grades should reflect achievement and that behavioral issues should be handled behaviorally.*

> *The students were studying world cultures and geography, and an important culminating assignment came at the end of the year. Students worked in groups of four. Each student was to select a region (South America, northern Europe, the Mediterranean area, Africa, Russia and Eurasia, southwest Asia, and so on) so that topics among the four students would represent geography and cultures from around the world. Each student was responsible for his or her contribution, but then the group was to work on a coordinated class presentation on the question "How has the geography of these regions influenced the cultures within it?" This central question reflected the learning goal for the assignment and was derived from the general curriculum standard "Students apply geographic knowledge and skills to address cultural, economic, social, and civic implications of living in various environments."*

> *When the other students in his group were presenting, Jayden distracted the class by pulling faces that indicated boredom, lack of interest, and disrespect for their presentations. Then for his own portion of the presentation, Jayden delivered a stand-up comedy–style speech mocking his chosen region. Mr. Miller was furious.*

> *Rather than throwing the book at Jayden and assigning him an F for his performance, Mr. Miller took a different tack, consistent with his belief that grades should reflect achievement and that behavioral issues should be handled behaviorally. In a conference with Jayden, he admitted that the outrageous performance was funny. However, he pointed out that the performance belittled the people and the region he was supposed to be studying and, more immediately, wasted the time of his classmates, who were supposed to be learning something from his presentation.*

Mr. Miller asked Jayden if he would be willing to apologize to his classmates and ask them for another chance to help them learn about his region. If they accepted his apology, Jayden would get another chance to do a real presentation on his region. If they didn't, Jayden would receive an F. Mr. Miller acknowledged that such an F would have been partly tied to behavior, which bothered him a bit, but he didn't think it was fair to the rest of the class to take even more of their time without giving them some choice in the matter. So that was the deal: take it or leave it.

Jayden took it. He apologized to the class, which he managed to do in a serious manner, although he did enjoy the attention it garnered for him. Mr. Miller reasoned that receiving attention for doing something good was better than receiving attention for misbehavior. Jayden quickly worked up another presentation, this time a serious one, and received a B. In fact, he probably would have done A work if he had taken more time, but that was something for Mr. Miller and Jayden to work on in the future. Jayden and his parents saw the B as a reflection of what he had learned, not an F that served as a punishment for misbehavior. His parents were already only too familiar with Jayden's bad behavior.

Worth noting about this story is the fact that Mr. Miller set up a situation that gave Jayden some control (self-determination) and in which appropriate, goal-directed effort (self-regulation) resulted in achievement and its corollary grade. Had Mr. Miller assigned an *F* for the original performance, Jayden would still have wanted self-determination and used self-regulation—but it would have been control over and regulation of bad behavior, unrelated to the geography and world cultures learning goals.

The point of this story is that students will always go for control. It's a matter of *what* they will control. If you set up grading policies, instruction, and assignments in such a way that students have some control and know that effort will lead to achievement, students are more likely to develop healthy and positive self-regulation strategies, because these strategies will accomplish something valuable.

Student Self-Regulation in Action

When you start your grading process by clearly communicating to students what exactly they are supposed to be learning, and when you support summative assessment with formative practice and feedback opportunities, everyone is clear on what needs to be done. Stiggins (2009) summarizes this approach as "no surprises and no excuses" (p. x). That motto is most important for teachers and students but extends to administrators, parents, and community members as well.

A good strategy for eliminating surprises and helping students control their own learning is to involve students in tracking their progress. Here are a few examples of how this might be done. Once you see the student self-regulation embodied in these classrooms, you should be able to come up with a whole range of adaptations of these strategies to fit your classroom, students, and subject-matter content.

Minute Math

A student teacher I once supervised invented "Minute Math," based on an idea from one of her education classes. I tell you this to give credit where credit is due and also to make the point that all teachers can do this type of work, regardless of their experience level. What it takes is a belief that the learning belongs to the students, that it is theirs to track, and that being in charge of tracking their own progress will engage them more in planning and using strategies to enhance their own learning.

In this case, having students track their own learning turned a rote memory task, memorizing multiplication facts from Ø through 10, into a lesson in "learning how to learn" as well. It was third quarter in third-grade math, and the main learning goal was for students to know the multiplication facts. Friday of each week, there was a hundred-problem, five-minute timed test.

My student teacher designed a bar graph with ten sections, one for each week. Within each week's section, there was space to draw a bar predicting what score students thought they would get and space right next to it to graph the actual score, which students did on Fridays right after they took their timed tests. Then they predicted what they would do on the following week's timed test, drawing that bar in the next space. Finally, they used planning sheets to say what strategies they had used that week (such as flash cards or studying at home), whether or not they thought these strategies had worked, and what strategies they would use in the upcoming week to accomplish their goal (their predicted score for the next Friday).

Students loved this—all students, not just the usual suspects. At the lower end of the achievement continuum, the few students who never did get 100 percent on the timed tests still were able to plan, accomplish, and see evidence of growth. At the upper end, the students who hit 100 percent in the middle of the ten weeks didn't want to stop, even though they had mastered the multiplication facts and achieved the learning goal. What they did was set new goals (such as "I can get 100 percent in four minutes, not five, next week!"). The accuracy of the students' predictions increased over the ten weeks, and most of the students, including all of the low achievers, expressed a mastery-goal orientation, wanting to learn for learning's sake (Brookhart, Andolina, Zuza, & Furman, 2004).

"I Can" Statements

Adams Elementary School in Spokane, Washington, was one of the pilot schools that tried out standards-based report cards and standards-based reporting practices a year before the rest of the schools in their district. The fifth-grade team at Adams consisted of three teachers, one first-year teacher and two experienced teachers. First, these teachers settled on the most important learning targets for grading. By *learning targets*, they meant standards phrased in student-friendly language so that students could use them in monitoring their own learning and, ultimately, understanding their grades.

One of the learning targets was "I can use decimals, fractions, and percent to solve a problem." The teachers listed statements for each proficiency level under that target and steps students might use to reach proficiency. As teachers gave assignments, students checked off for themselves where they were and conferred with their teachers about what they needed to do next. The results of this process were posted in the classroom, using the scale 4, 3, 2, 1. The 1 level was *not* failure but rather signified "I don't get it yet, but I'm still working."

Mary Weber (personal communication, July 22, 2010), principal of Adams Elementary at the time, reported that it might seem daunting to a student coming in that everyone's proficiency levels were posted in every classroom. But she said, "Kids knew what it looked like." They were able to look at a paper and answer the question, "Do you think this is a 4, 3, 2, or 1, and why?" They could use rubrics to help them. And most importantly, they did not perceive the *1* level (which was called "I don't get it yet") as punitive. Students began to work harder than teachers. Of course, the teachers had enabled that to happen by changing the classroom atmosphere so that it really was about learning and not about judging. So the teachers did some amazing work, too.

The usual recommendation is that grades not be posted where other students can see them (Brookhart, 2009a). It is a testimony to the complete switch from an evaluative classroom culture to a learning culture that posting progress helped students keep track of their own work in a supportive atmosphere. One of the mechanisms that allowed this to happen was that the posted "grades" were changeable, which contributed to self-regulation of learning. When students improved, they changed their progress levels on the post. These grades were not final sentences.

Reflective Tools

I have seen students at all levels, from first-graders in Title I reading to high school students, benefit from using reflective journals as vehicles for self-monitoring. I have also seen reflective journals not help at all with self-reflection and self-regulation. It very much depends on the atmosphere of the class—whether it's about learning or performing—and on the way the students and teacher handle the journaling.

Reflective tools can be for personal planning only, like a reflective journal, or they can be a part of formal progress monitoring. For example, students are often expected to fill in reflection sheets or provide captions for portfolio entries that include their thoughts on what they did well, how they still want to improve, and what their plans for improvement entail. Just like reflection in journals, this more formal reflection exercise can be handled in a learning-oriented way or a performance-oriented way. It depends on the atmosphere you create. If the emphasis is on learning and mistakes are seen as an opportunity to learn, then it will be safe for students to reflect on what needs improvement. If the emphasis is on scoring, mistakes become opportunities to lose points, and it is not safe to need improvement. A savvy student, then, will realize it's not good to be too honest about the whole "needs improvement" thing.

Self-reflection, in any of its forms, fits well with a standards-based approach to grading that emphasizes learning, relies heavily on recent evidence for grading, and offers opportunities for revision and showing improvement whenever possible.

Student Self-Regulation Through Practice

Formative assessment that offers students opportunities to practice and build competence before you "take stock" with a graded assignment also fosters student self-regulation. Strategy 3 in chapter 4 discusses the whole formative assessment process. Here, we simply highlight ways that employing formative assessment as a regular part of your instruction supports student self-regulation. During the formative process, students use self, peer, or teacher feedback to help them gauge what they can do and what they still need to learn. Then they can make decisions about where to expend their efforts accordingly.

Formative Opportunities in Performance Assessment

Assignments that require complex thinking and writing, constructing, or arranging materials (for example, locating and presenting several different recycling plans and describing how their methods and results are alike and different) are well suited for incorporating a formative process right into the assignment. That is because they can go through several stages of revision or refinement before being completed. Written work of all kinds (essays, stories, poems, term papers, themes, and so on) lends itself well to a cycle of drafts, self-assessment and feedback, and revision. Similarly, long-term projects of all kinds (science projects, building a bookcase, making a model of a battlefield or the solar system) lend themselves to monitoring and feedback along the way before the final project is finished and graded.

Formative Assessment Before Tests

Tests, unlike performance assessments, don't lend themselves to student revision. Unit tests and other on-demand assessments usually include at least some questions with right and wrong answers. There is no opportunity for feedback once students get to the point of taking a test. Once students have received a graded test back, they know what the answers should be, and so retaking the same test would not indicate achievement in the content domain but rather memory of specific answers. Allowing a retake of a graded test requires another form of the test with different questions about the same material.

A good way to provide formative opportunities for tests is to give practice quizzes along the way. Students can learn what specific knowledge and skills they still need to work on before you give the graded test. For even more practice with target concepts, give students your test blueprint—your plan for what the test will cover—and have students write the practice questions themselves. They will learn from both writing and answering the questions.

What About "Do-Overs"?

When I recommend supporting graded assessments with formative assessments, I am not advocating an endless stream of "do-overs." Resubmission is always Plan B. Plan A is that the students have enough opportunities for ungraded practice that the graded work, whether it's a test or final project, is an accurate and fair representation of their achievement of the learning targets. Provide substantive feedback, not grades, for formative assessments. That way, students will be more likely to interpret and use your feedback as information for improvement, which will head off the need for excessive do-overs. If you grade formative assessments, students will be more likely to interpret your feedback as information about why they lost points in the grade.

However, once you have embraced the formative impulse, it is tempting to allow summative, graded work to also become practice. ("If it's true that 'life is a journey, not a destination,' then isn't everything really formative and on its way to something else?" you might reason.) Students may ask for retake or do-over opportunities, especially as they get used to monitoring their own learning and becoming their own advocates.

Occasionally, you might want to allow for resubmission of graded assignments. This is most appropriate when, for reasons of illness or other emergencies, scheduling conflicts, or availability of materials, the graded assignment was due before the student was ready. It is also appropriate, on a case-by-case basis, for students who have genuine changes of heart about how they approach their work, perhaps because of coaching from you about their effort or behavior. It is best to have a clear policy about whether you will allow resubmission of graded assignments, and if so, for what reasons.

Figure 3.1 is an example of the kind of policy you might decide to implement if you decide to allow for resubmissions. The suggested strategies are intended to help teachers take into account individual extenuating circumstances in the lives of students without placing an unreasonable burden on teachers' time. Above all, they are designed to support grading that reflects achievement after opportunity to learn.

In this class, you will have at least one opportunity for practice and feedback that does not count in the final grade for a standard before you have a test or other assessment that does count toward your final grade. Requests to resubmit graded work will therefore be very rarely honored.

If absence, illness, and/or family emergencies have caused you to miss practice work, you should ask to make up that work before you take a test. It is preferable to negotiate a later test date than to take a test for which you are not prepared and then request a retake. Similarly, if absence, illness, and/or family emergencies have caused you to get behind on work for a graded project or paper, it is better to renegotiate the due date than to turn in work you know is not ready. I will make decisions about changing due dates on a case-by-case basis.

In unusual circumstances, you may ask to resubmit all or part of an assignment or to retake a test.

If you want to resubmit all or part of an assignment or retake a test, you should discuss it with me outside of class time. You should be able to explain what work you want to redo and why.

I will base my decision on your individual circumstances, including how you used class time and your work on other assignments.

If I do honor your request to resubmit a project, paper, or other assignment, I may ask for resubmission of all or part of the assignment, depending on the reason for the resubmission.

Retaking the same test again after it has been returned to you is not possible. If I honor a request to retake a test, I may ask you either to take a different test over the same material or to do an equivalent assignment.

Figure 3.1: Sample classroom policy about resubmission of graded work.

Exceptions, Exemptions, Differentiation

I hope I have made the case that standards-based grading helps a wider range of students than does traditional grading, which tends to privilege the winners (the *A* and *B* students) and leave the others in the dust. The reason for this is that grading on achievement of standards for learning provides meaningful information to all students, and information is power. Once you have reformed your grading practices to grade on achievement, you are closer to keeping the promise of learning for more students. However, some students will still need exceptions, exemptions, or differentiation.

Differentiated Instruction

Differentiation for most students should be accomplished via instruction, not grading. In most differentiated instruction, the standards for learning do not change. What change are the instructional methods and materials that give students access to these standards and opportunity to learn them. Differentiated assessments *of the same standards* can be used and do not change grading, which is done according to the strategies listed at the end of this chapter and detailed in chapters 4 and 5.

For example, a middle school student with a reading disability may be able to meet the same standards in American history as her classmates if she uses audio materials in place of most of the reading materials. Her grades (for example, proficient) on each history standard would be arrived at in the same manner as her classmates' grades, without penalty for the accommodations in instruction or assessment.

Another student in the same American history class may already know and be able to do many of the things required for proficiency on the standards. At the beginning of the unit, the teacher may help the student demonstrate these understandings and capabilities via a pretest. The teacher and student may agree on some curriculum compacting. For some lessons, the student joins the class. During other lessons, he pursues work at the advanced level, offering him the opportunity to learn extended and enriched knowledge and skills on those same standards. Assuming he is successful with this work, his grade reflects his advanced performance on the standards.

Standards-Based Grading in Special Education

While some have wondered how standards-based grading can apply to special education, in fact it offers the opportunity for more meaningful reporting than some of the special education grading practices that have been adopted in traditional grading contexts. Traditionally, teachers have used a variety of grading practices for special education students (Bursuck et al., 1996), many of which students did not perceive as fair (Bursuck, Munk, & Olson, 1999). Many of these practices mixed information about student achievement of learning goals with information about student effort and improvement and resulted in uninterpretable grades.

Jung (2009; Jung & Guskey, 2007, 2010) uses a model for standard-based grading practices in special education that is designed to result in grades that yield meaningful information. First, she reminds special education teachers that the distinctions between *product* criteria (achievement or proficiency levels on learning standards), *process* criteria (effort and work habits), and *progress* criteria (improvement or growth), still apply in the case of special education (Guskey & Bailey, 2001). *Product criteria* are what I have termed "student achievement of intended learning outcomes," and I use that phrase because it emphasizes achievement and learning. The promise of learning for all students is a theme of this book. The concepts are the same; both refer to a student's current achievement status.

Jung's model then lists five steps for reporting achievement of intended learning outcomes for special education students (Jung, 2009; Jung & Guskey, 2007, 2010).

1. **Determine whether accommodations or modifications are needed.** If students can reach grade-level standards with *accommodations*, defined as differentiation in instruction and assessment methods that does not alter the standards, then no changes in grading are required. If students require *modifications*, defined as changes that alter the standards, these altered standards are listed in the student's individualized education program (IEP).

2. **Establish standards for modified areas.** The IEP team determines what the modified standard is, what annual goals and short-term objectives should be for this student, and how the modified standard links to the grade-level standard.

3. **Determine the need for additional goals.** For some special education students, additional goals, like behavior or mobility, may be important. These goals are listed in the IEP, are monitored, and are reported in a supplement to the standards-based report card.

4. **Apply fair and equitable grading practices to appropriate standards.** When students' accommodations allow them to be graded on the same standards as their grade-level classmates, apply the same grading practices as for their classmates. When modifications have

resulted in altered standards, apply standards-based grading practices to the altered standards.

5. **Communicate the meaning of grades.** Note on the report card when a grade was based on a modified standard. Attach to the report card a brief supplemental document explaining the student's learning goals and how they relate to the grade-level standard. As for other students, report process criteria such as behavior, effort, and work habits separately.

Jung and her colleagues have been implementing this model with teachers since 2009. The preliminary results are promising. Guskey, Swan, and Jung (2010) summarize the findings to date:

- All parents interviewed preferred this model of reporting over the traditional reporting methods. Parents felt they received more and clearer information on how their children were performing and on the level of work they were able to complete.

- General education teachers felt that this grading model was a little more work than their traditional grading practices. However, they felt the extra work was worth it because the outcome was better communication.

- General and special educators agreed that the model required that they communicate about students' progress. Both general and special educators felt that, by using this model, they had a better understanding of the student and of each other's expectations.

- Fewer teachers used the model than the researchers might have liked. Jung (personal communication, August 20, 2010) thinks this is because teachers don't know how to modify general curriculum standards, and they need more support to be able to do this.

These findings specifically suggest that the model offers a solution to the problem of grade meaning that has heretofore vexed special education (Bursuck et al., 1996). The model fits nicely with the grading practices advocated in this book for all students, which are based on reporting achievement of intended learning outcomes. Therefore, it is the model I recommend for grading in special education.

Twelve Grading Strategies

By now I hope it is clear that the same grading strategies that support motivation also support learning and clear communication about what has been learned. Figure 3.2 summarizes twelve grading strategies that, when taken together and used consistently over time, will accomplish all these purposes. The strategies are listed in the order in which they will be discussed in detail in chapters 4 and 5.

Strategies for Grading Individual Assessments

1. ***Communicate clear learning targets.*** Make sure students clearly understand the learning targets and the criteria on which they will be assessed.

2. ***Make sure assessments are of high quality.*** Make sure that each assessment and its scoring or grading criteria deeply match the learning targets to be assessed, representing the range of requirements for both content knowledge and thinking skills.

3. ***Use formative assessment.*** Support summative (graded) assessments with formative assessments. Help students see the connection between their effort and their achievement.

4. ***Inform students.*** Give students the information they need to plan, study, and achieve.

   a. Announce tests ahead of time. Let students know the material the test will cover and how they might study.

   b. Give due dates for graded projects, papers, or other performance assessments at the time of assignment.

5. ***Grade achievement, and handle behavioral issues behaviorally.*** Use other management strategies (not grading) to handle nonachievement factors.

6. ***Grade individuals.*** Assess individual achievement (no group grades).

Strategies for Assigning Report Card Grades

7. ***Grade on standards.*** Base grades on standards of achievement of intended learning outcomes.

8. ***State grading policy clearly.*** Have a clear grading policy, and share it with students and parents.

9. ***Keep standards-based records.*** Keep records of individual assessment results by standard (or standards-based learning goals).

10. ***Use multiple measures.*** Use a variety of assessments for each learning goal that, taken together, represent the domain well.

Figure 3.2: Grading strategies that support and motivate student learning.

continued →

11. ***Maintain standards-based meaning when blending evidence.*** Combine grades from individual assessments to reflect achievement of standards-based learning goals.

  a. Weight evidence according to its importance for the learning goal, giving proportionally more weight to recent, clear, and reliable evidence.

  b. Make sure your calculation or judgment method is not undermined by characteristics of your scores or scales (for example, do not use zeros in a percentage-based system, transform rubrics and percents into an equivalent scale before combining, use the median if you "average").

12. ***Involve students.*** Engage students in establishing grading policies and tracking their own learning progress.

All of these strategies support grading on achievement of intended learning outcomes. All of these strategies support student effort and motivation as well. As clearly as summary grades can, grades that you derive by using these strategies will provide valid information about learning to students, parents, and the school.

Summary

One big idea in this chapter is that grading on achievement also supports student effort and motivation. Giving students opportunities for ungraded practice and allowing them to track their own progress are important motivational strategies and are best done before final, graded assessments. Teachers should have clear classroom policies about redoing graded assignments or tests to keep these requests manageable. A second big idea is that learning-focused grading is also possible for special education, and Jung's model of how to do that matches with the more general recommendations in this book. Finally, figure 3.2 outlines the specific strategy recommendations that form the core of the "how-do-do-it" advice in this book.

Part 2

TWELVE GRADING STRATEGIES THAT SUPPORT STUDENT LEARNING

Chapter 4

Designing and Grading Assessments to Reflect Student Achievement

Individual assignment grades are the "ingredients" on which you base the report card grade. If individual assignment grades are not sound, the final grade won't be, either. The negative way to say this is "Garbage in, garbage out." What you should be aiming for is "Good stuff in, good stuff out." The strategies I will explain in this chapter and the next (outlined in figure 3.2, page 37) will enable you to deliver the good stuff.

Strategy 1: Communicate Clear Learning Targets

> Ms. Thomas taught elementary social studies. One day, her students read about different explorers and filled in graphic organizers about the passages they read. They recorded such information as the explorers' names and dates, where they were from, where they explored, and what they hoped to accomplish (according to the textbook). The principal visited Ms. Thomas's classroom on a subsequent day and asked some students, "What are you learning?"
>
> "We're learning this stuff," one student said, as he pointed to the graphic organizers.
>
> "And we're reading this book," said another student.
>
> "How will you know when you have learned these things?" asked the principal.
>
> "We'll know when we get our tests back," said the first student.
>
> "Yeah, and if the teacher likes our worksheets," said the other.

Unfortunately, this story describes a lot of students. They can tell you what they are doing, but not what they are supposed to be learning. Consider another subtly but profoundly different version of this scenario.

> Ms. Thomas taught elementary social studies. She started her unit on explorers with a brief discussion about "beginnings" and how much fun it can be to find out "how things got to be the way they are." Then she said, "There are two important 'how things got to be' that this unit will help you learn. First, you'll learn why

some European countries wanted to colonize parts of the world they had never seen. And second, you'll learn how some science and technology developments, like the compass and the sextant and some others, made this possible just at the same time as these countries wanted to explore and colonize."

One day, her students read about different explorers and filled in graphic organizers about the passages they read. They recorded such information as the explorers' names and dates, where they were from, where they explored, and what they hoped to accomplish (according to the textbook). The principal visited Ms. Thomas's classroom on a subsequent day and asked some students, "What are you learning?"

"We're learning what European explorers did during the 1400s and early 1500s," one student said, as he pointed to the graphic organizers.

"How will you know when you have learned these things?" asked the principal.

"We'll know when we can summarize what they all hoped to accomplish in a couple sentences," the student replied.

"Yeah, and when we have enough information to make a table so we can compare their dates and places," another student added.

The first learning target, being able to explain why some European countries wanted to colonize parts of the world they had never seen, is within sight for these two students. No doubt the second learning target, understanding the contributions of science and technology to this period in history, will be within sight for these students when the time comes. What a difference!

Identifying Learning Outcomes

Spelling out learning goals clearly is the key to standards-based instruction and assessment. Obviously, you can't teach to a standard unless you can define it for yourself and your students. So the first step in designing assessments to reflect student achievement is to state clearly what that achievement should be. We have already discussed how learning goals should be derived from state content standards and curricular goals.

Teacher goals and instructional objectives are one step short of being learning targets for students. If grades are to be meaningful, they must be based on learning targets that students understand (Moss & Brookhart, in press). Teachers make learning outcomes clear to students in the following ways:

- Stating the outcomes in student-friendly language via words, pictures, actions, or some combination

- Using examples of good performance when possible

- Making desired outcomes concrete by using activities and assignments in which students can clearly see that their performance demonstrates understanding

- Establishing criteria for what good work looks like

Only then does an instructional objective become a learning target that students can really aim for.

A learning target is the student's-eye view of the standards on which you will grade—what the student should be trying to reach. If students clearly understand what they are to learn and how they will be evaluated, they can exercise some control over their study and work.

If students don't understand what they are to learn, then at best, dutiful students will comply with your requests because you're the teacher. We are all only too familiar with what this sounds like ("I'm not sure what she wants"). Students will experience grades as general ratings of themselves personally, not information about what they have learned. They may become apathetic or anxious. This is not only demoralizing for students but means the teacher is doing the lion's share of the work.

"You Mean if I Learn This, I'll Get an A?"

Administrators in the Armstrong School District in Pennsylvania work with teachers in their buildings on sharing learning targets and criteria for success with students. After a year of focusing on learning targets in her building, an assistant principal in one of the high schools was amazed at the changes in both teachers and students. During an administrative team meeting, she reported:

> One of the teachers who did the induction program shared this example of what happened during a discussion of the learning target and success criteria. A student said to the teacher, "You mean if I learn this, I'll get an *A*?" It's like we are finally sharing the secret with our students! All of this—the meetings, our discussions and monthly clarifications—has been so very helpful for me. (Personal communication, February 24, 2010)

"You mean if I learn this, I'll get an *A*?" is the realization we want all our students to have. You can see the beginnings of self-regulation in the way the student spoke. He, not the teacher, was going to do the learning. And he would get an *A*, not be given one. This agentive, cause-and-effect reasoning on the part of students is what internal motivation looks like in the classroom.

What Next?

Of course, after you have clearly stated the intended learning outcomes that will be the focus of your grades and restated or presented them as student-friendly learning targets so the students understand what to aim for, you will need to teach this knowledge and/or these skills. Researchers have found that clear learning goals and lessons that are coherent with those goals are positively associated with three outcomes: (1) students' perceptions of their classrooms as supportive of learning, (2) students' reports of self-determined learning motivation, and (3) the development of competence (Seidel, Rimmele, & Prenzel, 2005).

As discussed in the previous chapter, part of coherent instruction is offering students formative assessment opportunities that will allow them to practice and to gauge their performance against the standards you will ultimately use to grade them. At some point, it will be time to take stock, to summarize what students have learned, with a graded assessment. So we turn now to the topic of how to make sure these graded assessments actually do tap the intended knowledge and skills. You're not really grading on achievement of learning outcomes if your assessments don't tap them.

Strategy 2: Make Sure Assessments Are of High Quality

Mr. Jones taught middle school science. He used quizzes and tests to see whether students learned the material in the textbook or from class demonstrations. He did a unit on hurricanes, and the unit test consisted of fill-in-the-blank questions asking about the names, parts, stages of development, and rating system for hurricanes. All of these were recall-level questions. During common planning time with the other teachers on his team, he noted to them that this year he was also adding a performance assessment, so that there would be two final grades for the unit, not just the one test that measured memory of hurricane facts. He described what he had in mind for the new assessment: "The kids are going to make posters. I'm going to have them pick a hurricane in history, like Hazel in 1954 or Katrina in 2005. They'll put information about them on posters, and we'll put the posters up all around the room."

Unfortunately for his students, the "performance skills" they could show in this assessment were poster-making skills. The science content, information about hurricanes, was still just facts. Instead of being written on a test or quiz, the facts were written or drawn on posters. The grades Mr. Jones would assign would still represent recall and reproduction of facts, not higher-order thinking—unless you count poster design, which is not part of the science standards he was trying to grade. A performance assessment that truly required application of the science skills might require following newspaper accounts of the famous hurricanes and explaining the hurricane stages and ratings the meteorologists were working with, how those led to the predictions at various points during the hurricanes' development, and how they explained the damage that ultimately resulted.

Assessments and graded assignments must match both the content and the thinking skills you intend for students to learn. If you want to assess whether students can recall or recognize definitions of vocabulary words, for example, you can ask them to match words with their definitions. If you want to assess whether students can comprehend text in which those vocabulary words appear, however, you have to ask them to read and answer questions that indicate their understanding. And if you want to assess whether students can use those vocabulary words themselves, in writing or speaking, you have to ask them to write or speak.

Writing Good Test Items and Performance Assessment Tasks

Poor test items and performance tasks don't tap the knowledge and skills you intend. Poor test items yield scores and grades that are a better indicator of test-wiseness than of learning. Poor performance assessment tasks yield scores and grades that are a better indicator of such factors as artistic talent, parental help, and copying.

A book on grading can't provide a complete treatment of how to construct high-quality assessments (see Nitko & Brookhart, 2011; Stiggins, 2008). Using high-quality "ingredients" for grading is so important, though, that I'll present some basics.

Here are two resources to get you thinking about how the test questions and performance assessment tasks you write (as well as the scoring systems you use, but we'll take that up later) are directly related to the quality of the information you'll get when you grade students' performance. Figure 4.1 lists dos and don'ts for writing good test items.

General

1. Use clear, concise language.
2. Prepare a draft and proofread it from a student's point of view.
3. Test important ideas, not trivial points.
4. Write short, clear directions for all sections of the test.

Figure 4.1: Dos and don'ts for writing good test items.   continued →

5. Don't copy statements from a textbook.

True/False Items

1. Make statements definitely true or definitely false.

2. Keep statements short, and make "trues" and "falses" about the same length.

3. Have only one idea per statement.

4. Use positive statements. If a statement contains a *not*, highlight it.

5. Avoid patterns of answers (for example, TTFF or TFTF).

Matching Items

1. Number the items in the first column; letter the response choices in the second column.

2. Make items and response choices homogeneous, with each response a plausible choice for any item in the set.

3. Keep the lists short (five to ten items).

4. Avoid "perfect" matching, where the last answer doesn't require a choice (that is, either provide more responses than items or specify that each response can be used more than one time).

5. Put longer phrases in the left column and shorter phrases in the right (response) column.

6. Arrange responses in logical order, if there is one (for example, if the answers are years, arrange them that way: 1945, 1950, 1972, 1986, and so on).

7. Avoid using incomplete sentences as items.

8. Keep all items and response choices on the same page of the test.

Completion/Fill-In Items

1. Don't put too many blanks together.

2. Make the answer a single word, if possible.

3. Make sure there is only one way to interpret the blank.

4. Use a word bank if total recall is not important.

Multiple-Choice Items

1. The stem should ask or imply a question.

2. If the stem is an incomplete sentence, alternatives should be at the end.

3. If "not" is used, highlight it.

4. Avoid statements of opinion.

5. Avoid linking two items, making the answer to one dependent on the other.

6. Avoid clueing (meaning that one item gives away the answer to another).

7. Use three to five functional alternatives (options, answer choices).

8. Phrase all alternatives so that they will seem plausible to those who are truly guessing.

9. Put repeated words in the stem, not in the alternatives.

10. Punctuate all alternatives correctly, given the stem. For example, if they are sentence endings, all choices get a period at the end.

11. Put the alternatives in logical order, if there is one.

12. Avoid overlapping alternatives; make each choice different from the others.

13. Avoid "all of the above" as an alternative.

14. Use "none of the above" sparingly—and sometimes, as the correct answer.

15. Adjust the difficulty of an item by making the alternatives more or less alike. The more similar the alternatives, the more difficult the item.

Restricted-Range Essay Items (one to three paragraphs per answer)

1. Use several restricted essay questions on a test, rather than an extended one.

2. Ask for a focused response to one point.

3. Specify in the question what sort of response is required. That response should include some critical thinking, not just recall, for example:

   a. Explain causes and effects.

   b. Identify assumptions.

   c. Draw valid conclusions.

   d. Present relevant arguments.

   e. State and defend a position.

   f. Explain a procedure.

   g. Describe limitations.

   h. Apply a principle.

   i. Compare and contrast ideas.

4. Use clear scoring criteria.

5. Don't use optional questions (on a test—longer essays that are performance assessments can include student choice).

Extended-Range Essay Items (longer than three paragraphs)

1. Use to test in-depth knowledge of a small range of content.

2. Call for students to both express and organize ideas. Specify what should be discussed and how it should be discussed.

continued →

3. Allow enough time for students to think and write.

4. Assign the essay as a paper or theme if out-of-class time is needed, if students are given a choice of topics, or if additional resources are required.

Source: Brookhart, 1999b.

Figure 4.2 provides a checklist for evaluating your performance assessment tasks.

1. Does the task require students to use all important content and thinking skills in the learning targets or standards you intend to measure?

2. Does the task require the student to perform (do, make, demonstrate) something, rather than just explain how to do it or reproduce information?

3. Does the task fit with the rest of your instruction and assessment of these learning targets or standards? For example, is the time and effort required to perform the task commensurate with the amount of emphasis it has in your overall instruction and assessment plan?

4. Are your directions clear? Would it be clear to students what aspects of the task are required, where choice is allowed, what explanation is expected, and so on?

5. Are the criteria and bases for evaluation clear? Do students know how they will be evaluated on the task?

6. Have you built in appropriate points for formative evaluation as students are working on the task?

7. Do all students in the class have access to appropriate resources needed to accomplish the task?

Figure 4.2: Checklist for evaluating performance assessment tasks.

Getting the Balance Right

Make sure your tests and performance assessments represent the content domain and levels of thinking you want students to learn, each in the right proportion. More important aspects of the content—those that required more instructional time and student work—should form more of your assessment than less important aspects. Your tests or performance assessments should balance recall and higher-order thinking in the proportions you intended for your students. You control this balance for a test when you first plan and then write the test items. You control this balance for a performance assessment when you plan and write the task and then write rubrics or a scoring scheme that scores content and thinking in the intended proportions.

The most common tool for planning assessments is an assessment blueprint. An assessment blueprint indicates the balance of content knowledge and thinking skills that a set of assessment items or tasks will cover. You can plan an assessment to achieve the desired emphasis and balance among aspects of content and levels of thinking, so you can have confidence that your individual assessments do measure this learning and you can interpret the resulting grades accordingly. Figure 4.3 shows a blueprint for a fifth-grade assessment on the water cycle. There are other formats for test blueprints you can use, too (see Nitko & Brookhart, 2011).

Intended Learning	Knowledge	Comprehension	Application	Total Points	Percentage
Understand that water moves in a continuous cycle		5		5	20
Understand the stages of the water cycle	4	6	10	20	80
Total Points	4	11	10	25	
Percentage	16	44	40		100

Figure 4.3: Blueprint for a fifth-grade unit assessment on the water cycle.

The first column lists the major learning goals the assessment is intended to measure. This list is as simple or as detailed as you need. The column headings across the top list the classifications in the cognitive domain of Bloom's Taxonomy. Any other taxonomy of thinking skills could be used, as well. The cells in the blueprint indicate the number of points allocated, and it is this feature of the blueprint that allows you to see how much each content standard and thinking skill contributes to the total score, as you can see by totaling across the rows and down the columns. Therefore, the blueprint describes the composition and emphasis of the assessment as a whole, so you can interpret the meaning of the test score accurately. It is not necessary for every cell in the blueprint to be filled. The important thing is that the cells that are filled reflect your learning goals. In addition to being the tool by which you match a test to the standards it is supposed to measure, the test blueprint simplifies test writing. It is much easier to make a blueprint and write test items to match it than to stare at a blank screen and just write a test.

The points describe the score, not the items. The ten points under "Application" in the row "Understand the stages of the water cycle" could be ten one-point multiple-choice questions, two five-point open-ended questions, or any other combination that makes ten points.

Conventionally, assessment blueprints are used for planning tests. Performance assessments also need "blueprint thinking," however. For our fifth-grade water-cycle unit, the two main objectives could also be assessed with a performance assessment task that asked students to diagram and explain the operation of the water cycle. Without actually drawing a blueprint (although you could), you could think to yourself that you wanted the performance assessment to have equal weight with the test, so that you had two different measures of achievement of the same learning goals. Thinking about how you want this performance assessment to be weighted relative to the test over the same learning goals is what I mean by "blueprint thinking."

Matching Instruction to Assessed Learning Outcomes

What do football players do? They practice the skills needed for the game, and then they practice playing games. What is the measure of their success? Of course—how they do on game day. Practice is not scored, it is coached; formative assessments are not graded, they receive feedback. The game is scored; summative assessments are graded. Players have clear ideas of how to execute the various skills, and they work on them to be able to deliver when it counts. In a similar fashion, make sure that what your students work on during instruction is the same knowledge and skills you intend to assess.

Using Scores That Reflect Levels of Achievement

Standards-based reporting requires that the "grades" themselves—the symbols you use to encode your grades' meaning—reflect levels of achievement of standards. If the intent is to blend scores from individual assignments for a report card that uses performance levels (basic, progressing, proficient, advanced) or level numbers (1, 2, 3, 4), then it is best to use those performance levels on the individual assignments, as well. There are two reasons for this. First, individual assignments graded in this way convey information about achievement in the same format as the report card. Parents and especially students can keep track of their progress. Second, it is easier to maintain meaning about students' achievement when you get to the stage of combining individual assignment grades into a report card grade.

The good news is that using scores that reflect levels of achievement of standards will also serve to focus students on what the standards mean. Poor rubrics that are just restatements of the directions for an assignment, and not descriptions of levels of quality, will not reflect levels of achievement. You have seen these—rubrics for a report that include, for example, a category that says "five points if an illustration is included, three points if it is included but hard to find or not labeled correctly, and one point if an illustration is missing." It's not that including an illustration is a bad thing. But performance on this rubric doesn't say anything about what the student learned. There are thousands of these rubrics in circulation, and more are being created every day. Let such rubrics be counterexamples for you as you move toward standards-based grading!

A good way to begin is to adopt a general rubric that you and others in your school agree describes general performance levels that coordinate with your state's accountability levels. Some states (Kentucky, for instance) have general rubrics that could be adapted for this purpose. You don't have to use the state performance-level descriptors verbatim. But your judgments of your students' level of achievement on the learning goals for instruction should share a common view of proficiency with the states' larger-sized (for example, "Reading") accountability judgments.

Figure 4.4 shows an example of a general rubric. The scoring rubric for a specific assignment would describe what each of the four performance levels looks like for the particular concepts or skills assessed by that assignment. For example, a geography teacher devised an assignment to teach and assess understanding of the effects of the movement of glaciers. This assignment provided a specific context for addressing the general standard "Knows the physical processes that shape patterns on Earth's surface." Students were to read about glaciers, view a video, and then select a specific location (for example, Alaska or Montana) to research in more depth. They were to prepare a report explaining the effects of glacial movement on the land forms in their location and how these effects were examples of the more general principles of glacial movement. The teacher adapted performance levels for this assignment from the general rubric. Her description of a level-3 (or proficient-level) performance was, "The student's performance shows a complete and correct understanding of the effects of glacial movement on land forms." (Note that this understanding might be partially demonstrated by including appropriate illustrations in the report and explaining them correctly. But unlike the rubric I criticized earlier, the rubric for this assignment focuses on the *quality of the learning*.)

The kind of rubric shown in figure 4.4 is called *holistic*, because one overall judgment is made about the quality of the performance, taken as a whole. Depending on the assessment, it may be more useful to use *analytic* rubrics, which have several different categories and describe performance levels for each one. To return to our glacier example, if the teacher wanted to use

Level	Description of Student Performance With the Concepts and Skills Intended for Learning
4—Advanced	The student's performance shows a thorough understanding of the concept(s), and extends understanding by relating this concept(s) to others or by offering new ideas about the concept(s); and/or the student's performance demonstrates the skill(s) at a high level.
3—Proficient	The student's performance shows a complete and correct understanding of the concept(s) and/or the student's performance demonstrates the skill(s) consistently.
2—Progressing	The student's performance shows an incomplete understanding of the concept(s) and/or the student's performance does not demonstrate the skill(s) consistently.
1—Basic	The student's performance shows serious misconceptions or lack of understanding of the concept(s) and/or the student's performance does not demonstrate the skill(s).

Figure 4.4: A general rubric that can be adapted for individual assignments.

the report to assess content knowledge about glacial movement, the skill of constructing an academic report, and writing, there might be three categories: understanding of the content, organization of the report, and written expression. Each category would have four performance levels. In this case, the teacher might weight the content rubric double (or triple), so that half (or three-fifths) of the total evaluation was about the geography and the other half about reporting skills. What categories you evaluate and how you weight them depends on the intended learning goal(s). Was report writing one of the things you intended your students to learn? Then it should be evaluated.

Figure 4.5 presents a checklist for evaluating scoring rubrics. Lack of attention to performance rubrics for individual assessments makes constructing meaningful summary grades for report cards difficult. Make sure rubrics for any given assessment are spot-on descriptions of performance quality that will help students, *and* make sure you know how they relate to the final grades you must use on the report card.

"But I don't always use rubrics," you say. "What about test scores? What about performance assessments with point-scoring schemes instead of rubrics?" It is fine to use points and percentages when they make sense. In a thirty-item multiple-choice test, for example, percentage correct is a logical metric. For some complicated assignments with scoring schemes that allot points for various aspects of the work, percentage correct is also a logical metric. For example, you could grade some science lab reports with points for the quality of various

1. Do the criteria (traits, scales) in the rubrics cover all important content and thinking skills for the learning targets or standards you intend to measure?

2. Will the number of performance levels serve your grading and reporting needs? Do you either use the same number of performance levels as for final grading or, if the performance quality is better described with a different number of levels, do you have a plan for translating performance into proficiency levels for final grading?

3. Do the maximum points for each criterion (after weighting, if appropriate) on the rubric match your instructional emphases and your learning targets or standards?

4. Do the performance levels clearly describe a wide range of achievement levels?

5. Is each performance level described in terms of observable characteristics of performance at that level?

6. Are the performance-level descriptions clear to students?

7. [If at all possible] Do you have examples of student work at each level of performance to illustrate the criteria for students?

Figure 4.5: A checklist for evaluating scoring rubrics.

aspects of each section—introduction, method, results, and conclusion—that you would then add and convert to a percentage.

Meaningful percentage-correct scoring requires a large number of items or points. A five-point quiz, for example, only yields scores of 0, 20, 40, 60, 80, or 100 percent. In a traditional grading context, that might be something like *F, F, F, D, B, A*. Such a scale is not likely to yield good information about the range of performance among your students. So do make sure you only convert to a percentage when there are a sufficient number of points for a meaningful scale.

In a traditional grading context, teachers enter percentages into the gradebook as percentages. In a standards-based grading system, especially if you need to mix percentage-based grades and rubric-based grades from individual assessments together for a report card grade, you first put them all on your performance-standard scale. To use percentage-correct scores in a standards-based grading system, you need to know what percentage constitutes proficient and all the other levels of performance. Often districts handle this by establishing cut scores on common assessments.

To some, establishing cut scores may sound new and unfamiliar, but it's really just a more thoughtful version of the same procedure that has been used in traditional grading for a long time (90–100=*A*, 80–89=*B*, and so on).

Those grade boundaries are cut scores, even though we're not used to thinking of them as such. Cut scores for individual assessments simply acknowledge the fact that some assessments are more difficult than others. A 90 on one assessment does not necessarily give evidence of the same level of proficiency as a 90 on another assessment. The question to ask is not "Who got a 90 or above?" but rather "What score would a proficient student be likely to get on this assessment?"

Strategy 3: Use Formative Assessment Before Grading

Hannah and Jason were in the same fifth-grade class. Their teacher always introduced new math concepts the same way. First, she would demonstrate, then she would have students do problem sets in class and for homework, and finally she would give a test. Hannah was a "natural" at math, and she usually responded to the class demonstration problems with a mental "Oh, I get it!" Off and running, she got all As on her class problem sets and homework, as well as her tests. Her teacher counted classwork, homework, and tests in approximately equal proportions in the final grade, and Hannah's final math grade was always an A.

Jason wasn't a natural like Hannah, but he worked hard, and he persisted until he caught on to the concepts and could solve the math problems. By the time of the test, he could pull an A just like Hannah, and he was very proud of himself for that. What a thrill to know as much as the "class brain"! His first two report card grades were Cs, reflecting the Fs and Ds he had gotten on the way as well as his As. By the end of the year, he had stopped working so hard. Why bother? He was going to get a C no matter what.

Jason's teacher did him a disservice. First semester, Jason *learned* that math! Second semester, he really didn't. But he could have, if his grades had reflected the learning he had accomplished by doing the classwork and homework. That first semester, he also learned another lesson, and it was that careful study and diligent effort devoted to learning math didn't really get him anywhere. Instead of helping Jason build a solid foundation of fifth-grade math concepts and equipping him for future success in math, his teacher sent him on to sixth grade less than well prepared and destined for a downward slide in math through middle school.

Less obvious, but equally true, is that the teacher did Hannah a disservice, too. While Hannah was pleased with her As, what she was learning was that she was a "brain" at math and that math didn't require any effort. She was not learning strategies to actually approach unfamiliar math concepts and learn them. No matter how "smart" she is, she will eventually hit a wall. In some future grade or math course, there will be some math content she is expected to learn that doesn't "just come" to her, and she won't know what to do.

Paradoxically, then, one grading practice that supports student effort and motivation is knowing when *not* to grade. On formative, practice assessments, give descriptive feedback (Brookhart, 2008), not grades. Formative assessments help students gauge their current performance against the criteria for success, so they know where they stand. Show students some good examples, some *A* work or proficient-quality work, and most of them will produce work of similar quality. Be sure to show a variety of examples so students see different ways to do good work. If you use only one example of good work—for example, using only one model paper to show how a student might explain reasoning on a math problem—students will just try to copy it.

As part of formative assessment, both student self-evaluation and teacher feedback should help students figure out what else they need to do, study, learn, practice, or otherwise work on before the summative, graded assessment. All of this should be coherent, and the formative (practice) and summative (graded) assessments should both require students to demonstrate the same knowledge and skills. What students are supposed to be learning, what they have the opportunity to practice, and what they are graded on should match.

Challenging Your Students

Using formative assessment also allows you to use work at the "moderate level of challenge" that we know is good for learning. In a nutshell, if students can't do the work yet, don't grade it. If they can already do the work, don't teach it.

By some estimates, about 40 percent of the work students do is work they already know how to do (Nuthall, 2005). As many students would say, "Borrrr-ing!" But think about it. If you teach in a context where about 80 percent correct, or its analog on rubrics or other scoring schemes, represents the pro-ficiency level, *and* if you grade even first attempts—for example, the first class-work or homework you give right after introducing a new concept—then you have to give assignments on which many if not most students can score about 80 percent with no prior experience. If you don't, "practice" grades will lower students' averages. Students who actually learn something and achieve profi-ciency they didn't start out with will look less than proficient in the final grade.

Connecting Effort With Achievement

You have communicated expectations to students. You have matched assess-ments to those expectations, and you have given students opportunities to practice, reflect on their performance, and improve before you give a graded, summative assessment. Take every opportunity to make the connection between effort and achievement explicit: "This exercise will help you learn how to prepare slides. Make sure you and your lab partner check slides prepared by both of you against the checklist, and keep working until you both know how to make a good slide the first time. On Tuesday, I'll observe slides at every lab station, and you will be graded." Not all students will be as persistent as Jason in our vignette and figure out for themselves how their practice makes their work better. Scaffold this learning with lessons that contain well-designed practice sequences and lots of reminders and encouragement.

Making Grades Meaningful

When students have done their best to hit a learning target, and their formative assessments indicate to them and to you that they are "getting it," then it's time to "take a grade," to use an expression from my teaching days. By this point, the students should understand what the grade means. Without this formative process—if the grades are not tied to a clear understanding of what was to be learned—students may have emotional responses to the grades they receive, but there is no basis for them to have productive responses to their grades in terms of further learning.

A very funny dramatization of this occurs in Sally Brown's "Coat Hanger Sculpture" monologue from the Broadway show *You're a Good Man, Charlie Brown*. Sally is Charlie Brown's little sister. A YouTube clip of a high school or college actress doing this monologue might serve as a good introduction to a more serious discussion (with students, parents, or colleagues) of standards-based grading principles. A dispirited Sally appears on the stage with a sad-looking coat-hanger sculpture—a sort of mobile. She has received a *C*, and she anguishes about it. "How can anyone get a *C* in Coat Hanger Sculpture?" she moans. What does the *C* mean? After some funny existential musing about the meaning of her *C*, and a lot of whining, Sally gets her teacher to change the grade. We side with Sally—but we never do find out what that *C* was supposed to mean.

Strategy 4: Inform Students

Mr. Martinez always gave homework in his high school American history class. He wanted to make sure all the students did the homework, but he didn't have time to grade 150 papers every day. So his strategy was that he would collect the homework sometimes but not other times, in a sort of random fashion. "Keeps them on their toes," is how he put it. One day he assigned students to read chapter 3 and answer the questions at the end of the chapter for homework.

The next day, Mr. Martinez collected those chapter questions from his first-period class. About two-thirds of the students had done the homework, and the other third hadn't. Those who hadn't received Fs for the assignment; the others received various grades, from A through F, depending on the quality of their work. Word spread, of course, and by fifth period, every student had something to hand in.

Even though all the students should have done the work, our concern here is that the grades that resulted from this exercise were essentially meaningless. Or more precisely, the grades that resulted were better measures of compliance than they were measures of what students understood about the contents of chapter 3 in their textbooks. In first period, an *F* for not doing the homework (whether for sound or unsound reasons) looked just like an *F* for doing the homework badly. In fifth period, it looked like all the students had attempted learning, when about a third of them had copied friends' work or rushed through the chapter themselves during lunch.

There are other approaches to homework that Mr. Martinez could have taken that would have increased the amount and quality of learning from that homework. The first and most important consideration, as we already mentioned, is designing homework assignments into the structure of a unit so that doing homework carefully actually does help students learn and perform well on final graded work. It is also productive to use self-monitoring strategies, whereby students keep track of the quality of their homework and other practice work to help them become more responsible for their own learning. One of the big problems in our scenario is that it set up Mr. Martinez to be the one responsible for catching students out. It was all about what he wanted and what he checked.

Helping Students Prepare for Tests

Pop quizzes are more exercises of authority than they are measurements of understanding. Pop quizzes on chapter-reading homework assignments penalize all the following students in the same way: those who read but still have questions, those who didn't read because something legitimate kept them from it, and those who didn't read because they were lazy or resistant. Worse, pop quizzes hold students accountable for knowledge and understanding before they interact with the material and you during instruction. Tests for which students are informed and can be prepared, if they choose, bring out the best in students. Self-regulated students can and will study. Students who don't study have made a choice, one from which you hope they will learn. But at least it was their choice, not yours.

Here's a sounder way to motivate students to read textbook chapters than threatening them with a pop quiz. Teach them the difference between literal and inferential questions, or recall and higher-order thinking questions. Ask them to read the chapter, then write and answer ten of their own questions—five literal or recall questions and five inferential or "thought" questions. You may need to coach a bit at first, so students don't just pick the first five facts in the chapter whether they're important or not. Writing and answering their own questions is more motivating than answering the text's chapter questions, because the students have some control over content and interest. Once students have written their questions and answers, have them share them and discuss why they chose the questions they did. What was interesting or important about those particular ideas? After this and several other lessons about the concepts in a chapter, with opportunities to figure out which concepts they find confusing and which are clear, students are ready to show what they know on a test for which they are given due notice and a description of what the test will cover.

Helping Students Plan Their Work

Just as you would announce a test ahead of time, you should give students the information they need to take charge of their learning on projects, papers, or other performance assessments. Announce due dates at the time of the assignment. Students can only plan and set goals—that is, use self-regulation strategies—if they have the information they need to do it. We all love to laugh at that sign over our colleague's office desk that says $\boxed{\text{PLAN AHEᴀᴅ.}}$ Setting a learning goal and working toward it, and then knowing you made it and it was your doing, is motivating. Getting stuck a day late and a dollar short is not.

Strategy 5: Grade Achievement, and Handle Behavioral Issues Behaviorally

> Lupe and Alexa liked school. In their eleventh-grade social studies class, Ms. Arnold assigned a report on the Great Depression. She gave the students directions for the report, including a choice of several different research questions about the period, the number and types of sources, and the form the report should take. Both Lupe and Alexa did excellent work, and both learned at about the same level as a result of doing the assignment. Ms. Arnold took off points for late work, however, and Lupe was absent the day the report was due. Lupe got an A-minus, and Alexa got an A.

The fact that the two friends' grades didn't reflect their learning was only the most immediate and obvious problem with this story. The report was a large part of their final grade, so the final grade did not end up reflecting learning accurately, either. Lupe's social studies grade affected her grade-point average and, because grade-point averages are used to rank students, indirectly affected the apparent achievement in her whole class.

Handling Nonachievement Factors

Strategies 1 through 4 have been about grading achievement. In this section, we turn to handling nonachievement-related issues in the context of an individual assessment. (Strategy 7 is about handling nonachievement-related issues in the final grade.)

The story about Lupe and Alexa illustrates that class participation, like other nonachievement factors—effort, work habits, and so on—should not be part of an individual assignment grade. For example, some project rubrics include a "participation" category. Or sometimes, grades are "docked" or points are reduced for work turned in late, as in our vignette. The resulting grade for a project, paper, or other work looks like it reflects achievement, but in fact is partly about nonachievement factors.

But if effort, behavior, and other nonachievement issues are not to be factored into a grade, what is to be done with them? Remember that assessment means collecting information. As a teacher, you collect all kinds of information about your students, and you use it. You notice that Arielle looks tired today, and if she looks tired every day for a week, you might call her home and ask about it. You see that Aiko is very interested in ballet and make a note to help her find some books about it. You notice that Tyrone never has a pencil with him, so you lend him a new one and extract a promise from him that if he will bring it every day for a week, he can keep it and you'll give him another. And so on.

My point here is simply to illustrate that even under traditional grading practices, we never graded *everything*, even if it seems we did. The recommendation to remove effort and behavior from grades is not as revolutionary as it sounds. And, frankly, believing that it is an important thing to do is part of being ready for implementing standards-based grading successfully.

Assess effort, interest, behavior, class preparation, attendance, prior experience and knowledge, current achievement, progress—anything you think will be useful information for teaching. Use much of that information formatively. Give students feedback on what you notice about them that will affect their learning, for good or ill. Help students build on strengths and improve weaknesses in study skills, effort, class preparation, and the like. Use rewards and punishments, behavioral contracts, consultation with parents, and other behavioral methods judiciously.

Figure 4.6 summarizes methods you can use to handle behavioral issues behaviorally. Use these methods instead of including nonachievement issues in grading. For example, in our story in chapter 3, Mr. Miller used a combination of coaching and a short-term contract with Jayden. These methods are also more immediate than grading. Therefore, with consistent use, they should be more effective than grades in addressing nonachievement issues.

Handle nonachievement factors (effort, interest, preparedness, cooperation, classroom citizenship, and so on) with the following methods:

- Offer formative feedback and coaching—work with the student.

- Draw up behavioral contracts.

- Use rewards and punishments judiciously.

- Make changes in seating arrangements or work space (for example, front or back of room, study carrel, library).

- Make changes in work partners (for example, change groups).

- Review learning expectations and consider differentiated instruction. (Sometimes students who misbehave or resist are really expressing frustration.)

Figure 4.6: Methods for handling nonachievement factors in the classroom.

Strategy 6: Grade Individuals

Erik and Carlos were excited about being placed in the same group for their final project in their middle school computer science class. Quade was also in the same group. Erik and Carlos did all the work, and they produced a really cool presentation that included 2-D animation they had programmed themselves. Quade was given the job of introducing the group's presentation before they showed it to the class. All three shared the A grade for the project. Erik and Carlos had As on their other assessments that term and got well-deserved As for the report period. Quade's A for the group project, averaged in with the Ds and Fs for his other assessments, resulted in a C grade for the report period. That C was the highest grade on his report card, and Quade's parents complimented him on his good work. "Who knows," thought Quade's dad, who had been worried about what sort of career his son might be headed for. "Computer science might be it!"

A grade should reflect the learning achievement and performance of the student whose grade it is. Given this book's two big ideas about grading—that grades should reflect student achievement of intended learning outcomes and that grading policies should support and motivate student effort and learning—the strategy of grading individuals needs little additional argument.

Assignment grades and report card grades are addressed to one student and family and are about that one student's learning.

You can—and should—give *feedback* to a group about how you see them working together, sharing responsibilities, listening, questioning, and so on. Do assess group performance (as opposed to ignoring it, or not assessing it), and use your observations and judgments about it to work with the group. Ultimately, the achievement the group is working toward should improve with improved group functioning, and that is your purpose for assessing and giving feedback about group functioning. Just don't confuse group process with the level of student achievement of subject-matter learning goals. It is vitally important that students learn communication and collaboration skills, which the Partnership for 21st Century Skills lists as a major category of learning and innovation skills (www.p21.org). Thus, formative assessment and feedback on these skills makes sense.

A good formative assessment technique for group work is to have students complete a peer evaluation form such as the one shown in figure 4.7. I would encourage you to design your own form, based on the way you do group work in your classroom. Design your form using input from students, and then— here's the important part—don't just pass out the form and then collect it. That kind of peer evaluation promotes "tattling" to the teacher and students' expectations that you will "do something" to unproductive or difficult group members. Rather, have students talk about their ratings and the process and express to one another how they might work together differently or better. This kind of peer evaluation fosters skills in group work.

	Student 1	*Student 2*	*Student 3*	*Student 4*
Helped set goals and plan work				
Listened to the suggestions of others in the group				
Contributed helpful suggestions to the group				
Carried out assigned tasks				
[Add categories in consultation with students.]				
Note: Directions should state how the cells are to be filled. Depending on the age of the students and how the group will discuss the results, cells could be filled by: (a) a checkmark or an X; (b) ratings, for example, 1 through 5; (c) rubrics, for example, 0=no, 1=sometimes, 2=usually; or (d) written comments.				

Figure 4.7: Peer evaluation form for formative use during cooperative learning assignments.

continued →

While you don't grade cooperative learning skills, you may want to assess and report them formally as well as coach them informally. In fact, you would probably do both—have students work on their group skills using formative tools like the one in figure 4.7 or other group activities—and then report students' cooperation and other learning-enabling skills on a special section of the report card, as shown in the example in figure 5.1 (page 67). Notice, though, that when you report cooperative learning skills, you still report the *individual's* cooperative learning skills.

Avoiding Group Grades

The corollary of "Grade individuals" is "Do *not* give group grades." Feelings of control over one's own learning and developing competence and belief in oneself as a learner are the primary internal motivators for students. Having one's grade depend on the work of others clearly works against these motivators. A student cannot control what his or her groupmate does. The student can help, but ultimately all a student can control is his or her own work and learning.

The research on cooperative learning supports the recommendation to assess individual achievement. One of the key principles of cooperative learning is individual accountability. In fact, Spencer Kagan (1995), one of the strongest proponents of cooperative learning, writes, "Every time I see group grades being used I am appalled. They are, in my view, never justified. Ever" (p. 68). Kagan goes on to explain his reasoning and lists seven arguments against group grades. His reasons are based on the fact that group grades depend, at least in part and sometimes in large part, on who the student's group members happen to be. Group grades, he argues: (1) are not fair, (2) debase report cards, (3) undermine motivation, (4) convey the wrong message, (5) violate the principle of individual accountability, (6) cause parents, teachers, and students to resist cooperative learning, and (7) may be challenged in court. On the contrary, the message you want your grades to send is what we have called in this book the "promise of learning." You want to set up your classroom so that students' efforts (their practice, study, and work on assignments) lead to learning, and you want grades that document that learning for students. From there, it is easy to coach students, showing them how the effort they expended resulted in learning.

But if not group grades, then what? Some alternatives to group grades are even worse than group grades themselves. Probably the worst story I have heard is that of a teacher who used group members' ratings of their groupmates' contributions to give "adjusted" group grades. She asked students to rate the amount and quality of each group member's contribution, using a 1–5 rating scale. She then averaged these ratings to rank the group members according to their peers' perceptions of the weight of their contributions, and then she weighted their grades accordingly. So if a group of three students did a *B*-level project, for instance, the strongest contributor might get a *B*+ or an *A* and the weakest a *B*– or a *C*, while the middle person would get a *B*. This strategy turns students into tattletales. What student would be motivated by ratting out a friend?

The alternative to group grades is to assess individuals, to see what they know and can do. Sometimes individual assessment can be part of a cooperative project, if the project has discrete parts and if each part is a representative indicator of what students know and can do. To assess whether students have met the learning targets a cooperative project addressed, you might ask them to write individual reflections or statements of learning ("What did I learn from this project?"), or you might assign a paper or give a test. Figure 4.8

1. Use a group project as an instructional activity, and then use an individual method (essay, paper, test, and so on) to assess the learning that resulted.

2. Structure a group project so that each individual contributes a discrete part of the end product (for example, different sections in a report).

3. After a group project during which all students create or do something together, ask each student to write a reflective paragraph or essay on what was the most important thing he or she learned, and why.

4. As students are presenting or displaying their group project, address oral questions to individual students about the project and their understanding of the underlying content. Make sure you have a broad enough set of questions. You might combine this method with one of the others.

5. As part of the project, have students come up with five (or whatever number you specify) group questions about what they think they are learning. Then ask students to write individual answers to these questions after they finish the group work.

6. Sometimes "group work" is essentially group practice with the facts or concepts to be learned, not a group project. These practice methods usually have individual assessment built in. Here is a partial list; see Kagan (1989/90) for more:

   a. Numbered heads together

   b. Three-step interview

   c. Think-pair-share

   d. Jigsaw

Figure 4.8: Ways to assess the learning of individual students from group work.

presents suggestions about how to assess individuals in the context of group work.

Summary

This chapter has described six strategies for grading individual assessments:

1. Communicate clear learning targets.
2. Make sure assessments are of high quality.
3. Use formative assessment before grading.
4. Inform students about when and how they will be graded.
5. Grade achievement, and handle behavioral issues behaviorally.
6. Grade individuals, not groups.

Only when the "ingredients" for the report card grade—the individual assessments on which the report card grade will be based—are valid indicators of student learning does the report card grade have a chance of also being a valid indicator of student learning over the report period.

Chapter 5

Designing Report Card Grading Policies to Reflect Student Achievement

While visiting my daughter in Los Angeles, I went to the natural history museum there. Imagine my surprise when, in one of the exhibits, I spotted a report card from the Los Angeles School District from the early 1900s. The real surprise was that it looked like it could have been a report card from the early 2000s. It was simply a list of subjects: reading, spelling, writing, arithmetic, and so on, with numbers (on the 0–100 scale) for grades. Traditional report cards have looked the same for over a century.

Before we go too far down the "grading policy" road, I want to go on record as saying that while the format of the report card is important, and you can do more with some report card formats than others, simply replacing subjects ("mathematics") with the names of standards ("numbers and operations") is not waving a magic wand that will automatically improve grading. Poor-quality indicators of achievement, or indicators of something other than achievement, can be put into standards-based report cards, and good-quality indicators of achievement can be recorded in more traditional formats. So when I recommend "standards-based grading," please understand that I am recommending that you put the standards-based *spirit* behind report card formats, the grade calculations for the report card, the assignments behind the calculations, and the instruction behind the assignments.

Standards-Based Report Cards

Standards-based report cards differ considerably and are more common at the elementary level than at the secondary level. One thing standards-based report cards typically have in common is that they have proficiency grades for achievement of standards and a separate indicator for behavior and work habits. Sometimes they also have indicators for growth.

The grading symbols for a standards-based report card can be handled in several different ways. Some standards-based report cards use the performance levels from the state's accountability system (Welsh & D'Agostino, 2009), such as basic, progressing, proficient, and advanced. Some standards-based reporting uses numbers, often 1, 2, 3, and 4, with 3 often meaning "proficient" or "meets standard."

Typically, standards-based report cards use the same number of levels for grading as their states use for accountability reporting. States currently use three to five performance levels on their state tests, with varying names (Perie, 2008). For example, Montana has four levels: novice, nearing proficient, proficient, and advanced. Most, but not all, states that have four levels use the third one to define proficiency. This can result in a paradox. When standards-based report cards are adopted, teachers sometimes say that there are "fewer As" (meaning fewer of the top-category marks, actually). The students who achieve simply what is required get a designation of proficient. Students must do something additional to get the advanced designation.

Lincoln Public Schools, Nebraska

The third-grade report card from the Lincoln Public Schools (fig. 5.1) reports achievement and behavior separately. I have selected it as an example because it includes a rubric for use with the behavioral indicators. This report card has a section called "Character Development," which reports overall behavior, and also a "Work/Study Habits" indicator for each subject. While evaluating "Character Development" sounds a bit like judging personality, in fact the descriptors in the rubric used for this section of the report card (fig. 5.2) are all observable behaviors.

Everett Public Schools, Washington

Figure 5.3 shows a fourth-grade standards-based report card (referred to as a "progress report") from the Everett Public Schools. Most of the standards statements on the report card use the same language as Washington State's Essential Academic Learning Requirements. However, to enhance communication about students' grade-level learning outcomes, in some cases the district has written reporting standards statements based on the state standards (Guskey & Bailey, 2010).

This report card covers three dimensions of student performance and gives each its own type of mark. One section of the card is devoted to "Behaviors That Promote Learning." Each trimester, teachers use a frequency scale to report their observations of how consistently students exhibit these positive work habits and other learning-related behaviors (*consistently, often, sometimes, rarely*). Then there is a section for reporting standards-based academic achievement, on a scale of 1 to 4 (*below, approaching, meeting,* or *exceeding performance expectations*). These are academic status measures. They answer the question, "How

	Q1	Q2	Q3	Q4
REPORT CARD Absences				

Student _____

Student ID _____

School _____

Homeroom Teacher _____

REPORT CARD
3rd Grade
Lincoln Public Schools
Year_____

Rev. 7/10

	Q1	Q2	Q3	Q4
Absences				

	Q1	Q2	Q3	Q4
Tardies				

ACADEMIC ACHIEVEMENT

4=Exceeds district standards   3=Meets district standards   2=Approaches but does not meet district standards   1=Does not meet district standards   •=Not taught/assessed this quarter

WORK/STUDY HABITS

4=Exceeds expectations   3=Meets expectations   2=Approaches expectations   1=Does not meet expectations
Indicators: Listens, Follows oral and written directions, Is on task, Participates in class, Strives for quality work, Seeks help as necessary, Completes assignments on time.

The descriptions below reflect the Lincoln Public Schools standards for this grade level. The marks given reflect quarterly performance.

CHARACTER DEVELOPMENT

	Q1	Q2	Q3	Q4
Selects and Uses Age-Appropriate Behavior • Accepts consequences for actions taken • Demonstrates self-discipline/control • Follows school and classroom rules				
Selects and Uses Age-Appropriate Coping Skills • Demonstrates decision making skills • Demonstrates organizational skills • Acts on the need for help				
Demonstrates Confidence in Self • Recognizes and accepts own abilities • Demonstrates a positive attitude toward self • Expresses personal feelings and ideas				
Interacts with Others Appropriately • Develops and maintains friendships • Demonstrates respect for individual rights • Works cooperatively with others				

Teacher(s) _____

MATHEMATICS

MATHEMATICS CONTENT	Q1	Q2	Q3	Q4
Numeration and Number Sense • Reads, writes, and compares whole numbers through 10,000 • Writes fractions • Rounds numbers to nearest 10 or 100 • Compares and orders decimals to hundredths				
Computation and Estimation • Adds and subtracts 3-digit numbers • Knows multiplication and division facts to 10				
Measurement • Tells time • Finds elapsed time • Finds perimeter				
Geometry • Uses properties of lines and angles • Plots ordered pairs				
Data Analysis and Probability • Collects, organizes, and interprets data • Interprets graphs • Uses probability to make predictions				
Algebra • Writes addition and subtraction sentences • Solves addition and subtraction work problems				

LANGUAGE ARTS

READING	Q1	Q2	Q3	Q4
Word Analysis/Spelling • Uses knowledge of advanced phonics patterns and multi-syllable word structures to read, write, and spell words				
Fluency • Reads grade-level text accurately with appropriate phrasing, expression, and rate				
Vocabulary • Builds knowledge of literary, content, and academic words • Applies context clues and text features to infer meanings • Identifies word relationships (e.g., synonyms, antonyms, multiple meanings)				
Comprehension • Identifies author's purpose • Retells information from narrative text including characters, setting, and plot • Summarizes main ideas from informational text • Uses prior knowledge to connect text to self, to other texts, and to the world • Monitors understanding and self-corrects when appropriate				
Multiple Literacies • Identifies, locates, and evaluates print and electronic resources to find and share information				
Work/Study Habits				

WRITING	Q1	Q2	Q3	Q4
Writing Process • Applies writing process to plan, draft, revise, and edit • Writes strong sentences using correct spelling, grammar, punctuation, and capitalization				
Writing Genres • Writes for a variety of purposes and audiences • Writes considering characteristics of a specific genre				
Handwriting/Publishing • Writes legibly and fluently • Publishes using electronic resources				
Work/Study Habits				

Figure 5.1: Third-grade standards-based report card from Lincoln Public Schools.

continued →

MATHEMATICS

MATHEMATICAL PROCESSES	Q1	Q2	Q3	Q4
Problem Solving				
Develops Conceptual Understanding				
Work/Study Habits				

Teacher(s) _____

HEALTH

HEALTH CONTENT	Q1	Q2	Q3	Q4
Mental/Emotional Health				
Communicable/Chronic Diseases				
Family/Social Health				
Consumer/Community/Environmental Health				

HEALTH PROCESSES	Q1	Q2	Q3	Q4
Uses Health-Promoting Skills • Makes decisions, sets goals, and accesses information				
Work/Study Habits				

Teacher(s) _____

SCIENCE

SCIENCE CONTENT	Q1	Q2	Q3	Q4
Dinosaurs and Fossils				
Energy				
Embryology				
Simple Machines				

SCIENCE PROCESSES	Q1	Q2	Q3	Q4
Uses Scientific Method • Observes, measures, and predicts				
Work/Study Habits				

Teacher(s) _____

SOCIAL STUDIES

SOCIAL STUDIES CONTENT	Q1	Q2	Q3	Q4
Communities Have a Place				
Communities Have a History				
Communities Have Responsible Citizens				
Communities Provide Goods and Services				

SOCIAL STUDIES PROCESSES	Q1	Q2	Q3	Q4
Uses Social Studies Skills and Knowledge • Acquires and analyzes information, communicates, and develops a historical awareness				
Work/Study Habits				

Teacher(s) _____

ART

	Q1	Q2	Q3	Q4
Thinks with Art • Integrates the 5 steps of the Creative Process				
Connects with Art • Reflects upon art in relation to history, cultures, and careers				
Communicates with Art • Uses the elements and principles of design with a variety of materials to communicate ideas through art				
Talks about Art • Looks at and talks about their work and the work of others using the language of art				
Work/Study Habits				

Teacher(s) _____

LANGUAGE ARTS

SPEAKING/LISTENING	Q1	Q2	Q3	Q4
Conversations and Presentations • Communicates ideas in classroom activities • Demonstrates presentation techniques and conversation strategies				
Listening • Listens in formal and informal settings for a variety of purposes				
Work/Study Habits				

Teacher(s) _____

MUSIC

MUSIC CONTENT (Skills)	Q1	Q2	Q3	Q4
Sings				
Plays Instruments				
Improvises & Composes				
Reads & Notates				

MUSIC PROCESS (Musicianship)	Q1	Q2	Q3	Q4
Elements of Music • Applies melody, rhythm, harmony, form, tone color and expressive qualities				
Work/Study Habits				

Teacher(s) _____

PHYSICAL EDUCATION

	Q1	Q2	Q3	Q4
Physical Skills and Movement Patterns • Combines skills and sequences in game-like settings				
Movement and Fitness Concepts and Principles • Identifies concepts of skills, fitness, and activities				
Health-Related Physical Activity/Fitness • Demonstrates cardiorespiratory endurance, muscle fitness, and flexibility				
Work/Study Habits—Personal and Social Behavior • Demonstrates fair play, cooperation, sharing, and respect for others				

Teacher(s) _____

TECHNOLOGY

	Q1	Q2	Q3	Q4
Creativity & Innovation • Plans and develops original products using technology tools				
Communication & Collaboration • Uses digital media and technology tools to communicate and collaborate				
Research & Information Fluency • Uses digital tools to gather, evaluate, and process information				
Technology Operations & Concepts • Selects and uses applications effectively and productively				
Work/Study Habits & Digital Citizenship • Actively attends to instruction and contributes to a productive learning environment • Understands and practices responsible, safe, & ethical uses of information and technology				

Teacher(s) _____

This report offers the best professional judgment about your child's performance in relation to school expectations. It is designed to convey a general view of your child's performance. A more specific report can be gained through a parent-teacher conference. Two conference days are scheduled each year. Additional conferences are welcome.

Source: Lincoln Public Schools, Nebraska. Used with permission.

	4 Exceeds District Standards	3 Meets District Standards	2 Approaches, but Does Not Meet District Standards	1 Does Not Meet District Standards
Selects and Uses Age-Appropriate Behavior	Follows classroom rules without prompting from the teacher Independently monitors own behavior Takes responsibility for own actions	Follows classroom rules with minimal prompting from the teacher Usually monitors own behavior independently Usually takes responsibility for own actions	Needs frequent prompting from the teacher to follow classroom rules Needs extensive support to monitor own behavior Does not accept responsibility for actions and may react in a defiant manner	Relies on constant redirection from teacher to follow classroom rules Is not able to monitor own behavior Does not accept responsibility for actions and usually reacts in a defiant manner when a request is made
Selects and Uses Age-Appropriate Coping Skills	Is persistent, knows when to ask for assistance Independently uses decision-making skills to make choices Is organized, completes quality work on time without teacher assistance	Is usually persistent, asks for assistance when needed Uses decision-making skills to make choices with minimal teacher assistance Is organized and completes quality work on time with minimal teacher assistance	Needs frequent teacher assistance to complete task Needs frequent teacher assistance with using decision-making skills to make choices Needs help organizing materials and needs frequent prompting to complete work	Needs extensive teacher assistance to begin and complete task Is unable to use decision-making skills to make choices without extensive teacher assistance Is unable to organize materials and complete tasks without extensive teacher assistance

Figure 5.2: Character development scoring guide, grades K–5, from Lincoln Public Schools.

continued →

	4	3	2	1
	Exceeds District Standards	Meets District Standards	Approaches, but Does Not Meet District Standards	Does Not Meet District Standards
Demonstrates Confidence in Self	Takes risks repeatedly even with occasional failures Is willing to try new tasks Is able to clearly state feelings and ideas without prompting	Will take risks often even with occasional failures Needs minimal encouragement to attempt a new task Frequently shares feelings and ideas with minimal prompting	Is unsure of own ability and needs frequent support to complete a familiar task Needs frequent encouragement and support to start a new task Will usually share feelings and ideas when prompted	Needs constant and intensive encouragement to attempt a familiar or new task Sometimes uses negative self talk Rarely shares feelings and ideas even when prompted
Interacts With Others Appropriately	Demonstrates leadership skills Shows respect for others Develops and maintains friendships with many classmates	Cooperates within a group Shows respect for others with minimal prompting Develops and maintains friendships with several classmates	Present in a group but needs teacher assistance to participate in a cooperative way Needs frequent reminders to be respectful of others Needs assistance to develop and maintain friendships	Observes but does not participate in group work Needs constant reminders to be respectful of others Needs extensive assistance to develop and maintain friendships

Source: Lincoln Public Schools, Nebraska. Used with permission.

Everett Public Schools			Student:		School:		page 1
Progress Report							
			Grade Level: Fourth Grade		Student ID:		
F = Fall	**W = Winter**		**S = Spring**		Year: 2009-2010 **Teacher:**		

Key for Academic Performance

4. Exceeding performance expectations at this time
3. Meeting performance expectations at this time
2. Approaching performance expectations at this time
1. Below performance expectations at this time
* Indicates *not evaluated at this time.*

ATTENDANCE	F	W	S
Days absent	1		
Days tardy	0		
Total days present	59		

KEY FOR BEHAVIORS THAT PROMOTE LEARNING

C	O	S	R
Consistently	Often	Sometimes	Rarely

SUPPORT SERVICES

Not enrolled in any programs.

TEACHER COMMENTS

Fall comments:

xxx is a very dedicated student. He completes all classwork on time. He is well liked by his peers. xxx is an advanced reader and I would like to see him challenge himself with more difficult text. xxx is doing well on his multiplication facts and problem solving in math.

Ensuring each student learns to high standards.

BEHAVIORS THAT PROMOTE LEARNING	F	W	S
—Cooperative Worker—			
Cooperates and interacts positively with others	C		
Participates actively and appropriately	C		
Respects property of school and others	C		
Respects rights, feelings and ideas of others	C		
Solves problems with peers effectively	C		
Follows school/classroom rules	C		
—Quality Worker—			
Shows willingness to try	C		
Shows persistence	C		
Keeps work space and materials organized	C		
Strives to produce quality work	C		
—Self-Directed Learner—			
Works independently	C		
Follows directions	C		
Completes classwork on time	C		
Returns home assignments on time	C		
Makes productive use of class time	C		
Reflects, sets goals, and evaluates progress	C		
Is prepared with materials and ready to work	C		

READING

	F	W	S
1. Understands and uses different skills and strategies to read	4		
Uses a variety of strategies (phonics, self-corrects, context)			
Uses vocabulary (word meaning) strategies			
Builds vocabulary through word parts, context, and reading			
Reads with fluency			
2. Understands the meaning of what is read	4		
Demonstrates evidence of reading comprehension with fiction texts			
Demonstrates evidence of reading comprehension with nonfiction texts			
Applies text components to comprehend			
Expands comprehension by analyzing, interpreting and synthesizing information and ideas in literary and information text			
Thinks critically and analyzes author's use of purpose and style			
Uses graphic organizers to show comprehension			
3. Reads different materials for a variety of purposes	4		
Reads to learn new information			
Reads to perform a task			
Reads to understand other cultures and perspectives			
Reads and uses resources to answer a question or solve a problem			
4. Sets goals and evaluates progress to improve reading	4		
Sets goals for reading			
Self-selects books at independent level			
States own progress in reading			
Explains what good readers do			
READING PROGRESS (+=significant, ✓=steady, –=minimal)	+		

WRITING

	F	W	S
1. Uses a writing process	3		
Pre-write, Draft, Revise, Edit and Publish			
2. Writes in a variety of forms for different audiences and purposes	3		
Writes to reflect, respond to literature, create stories, learn, explain, analyze information, and summarize			
3. Writes clearly and effectively			
Develops content appropriate to audience and purpose	3		
Develops organization appropriate to audience and purpose	3		
Develops style appropriate to audience and purpose	3		
Applies grade-level conventions (uses appropriate punctuation, spelling, capitalization and usage)	3		
Writes letters and numbers legibly: form, size, space, alignment (cursive and printing)	3		
WRITING PROGRESS (+=significant, ✓=steady, –=minimal)	+		

continued →

Figure 5.3: Fourth-grade standards-based report card from the Everett Public Schools.

Student: _____   page 2

COMMUNICATION | F | W | S

	F	W	S
1. Uses listening and observation skills to gain understanding	3		
2. Uses communication strategies and skills to work effectively with others		4	
Seeks solutions through discussing issues from different points of view			
3. Communicates ideas clearly and effectively		4	
Communicates clearly to a range of audiences for different purposes			
Uses media and technology in oral presentations			
COMMUNICATION PROGRESS (+=significant, ✓=steady, −=minimal)	+		

MATHEMATICS | F | W | S

	F	W	S
1. Two- and Three-Digit Multiplication		3	
Recalls basic multiplication and related vidsion facts through 10×10 quickly			
Develops fluency with whole-number multiplication			
2. Fractions, Decimals, and Mixed Numbers	*		
Solidifies and extends understanding of fractions and mixed numbers			
Develops an understanding of decimals, including their connection to fractions			
3. Concept of Area	*		
Develops an understanding of the spatial relationships of area and perimeter			
Solves problems involving perimeter and area of rectangles			
4. Additional Key Content		3	
Uses coordinate grids, finds simple probabilities, describes sets of data, determines elapsed time, determines basic measurement conversions, uses algebraic notation			
5. Reasoning, Problem Solving, and Communication		3	
Demonstrates strategic mathematical thinking and reasoning, using what is known, to solve problems			
MATHEMATICS PROGRESS (+=significant, ✓=steady, −=minimal)	✓		

SCIENCE | F | W | S

	F	W	S
1. Understands Scientific Concepts and Principles	3		
Properties and Change: Matter occupies space and has mass. Changes of state occur when matter is heated or cooled (Kit: Changes of State)			
Earth Systems, Structures, and Processes: The surface of the earth changes over time. Rocks and fossils provide evidence of change (Kit: Reading the Environment)	*		
Earth Systems, Structures, and Processes: Water has an important role in shaping the land. Humans interact with natural elements to affect changes in the landscape (Kit: Land and Water)			
2. Systems	3		
Analyze a system in terms of subsystems and large, more inclusive systems			
3. Inquiry	*		
Plan investigations, including field studies, systematic observations, models, and controlled experiments			
4. Application		3	
Work individually and collaboratively to design and produce a product to solve a problem			
Contributes to positive group activities by participating appropriately			
SCIENCE PROGRESS (+=significant, ✓=steady, −=minimal)	✓		

SOCIAL STUDIES | F | W | S

	F	W	S
1. Social Studies	3		
Civics			
Understands rights and responsibilities of citizens in the Washington State Constitution			
Understands how governments are organized into local, state, tribal and national levels			
Economics			
Understands how Washington State's economy is influenced by environment and population			
Geography			
Understands physical and cultural characteristics of regions in the Pacific Northwest			
History			
Uses multiple perspectives to learn about Washington State History			
Social Studies Skills			
Creates and uses questions to conduct research on an issue or event			
Uses multiple primary and secondary sources to find information and draw conclusions			
SOCIAL STUDIES PROGRESS (+=significant, ✓=steady, −=minimal)	✓		

FITNESS | F | W | S

	F	W	S
1. Fitness			
Demonstrates developmentally appropriate motor skills			
Demonstrates activity/sport specific knowledge and skills			
Evaluates health and fitness information			
Safely, actively, and appropriately engages in a variety of physical activities			
FITNESS PROGRESS (+=significant, ✓=steady, −=minimal)			

HEALTH | F | W | S

	F	W	S
1. Health	3		
Demonstrates understanding of nutrition, disease control, human body systems, growth and development, dangers of drugs/alcohol/tobacco, personal safety.			
Demonstrates understanding of how family, culture, and environmental factors affect personal health			
Demonstrates understanding of the impact of social skills on health			
HEALTH PROGRESS (+=significant, ✓=steady, −=minimal)	✓		

VISUAL ART | F | W | S

	F	W	S
1. Visual Art	3		
Demonstrates and applies visual art skills and concepts			
Uses creative process to develop ideas			
VISUAL ART PROGRESS (+=significant, ✓=steady, −=minimal)	✓		

MUSIC | F | W | S

	F	W	S
1. Music	3		
Demonstrates and applies music skills and concepts			
Contributes to positive group activities by participating appropriately			
MUSIC PROGRESS (+=significant, ✓=steady, −=minimal)	✓		

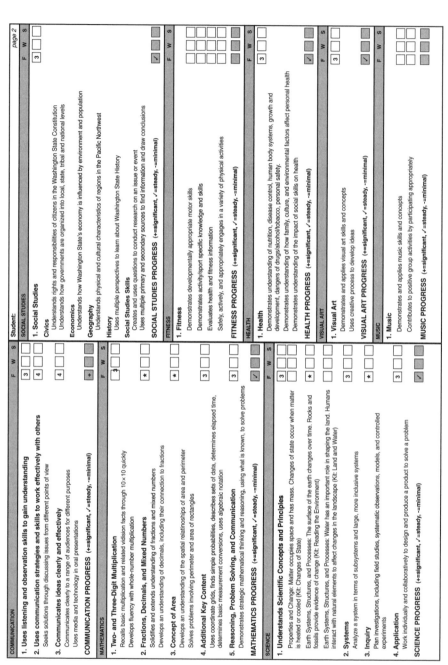

Source: Everett Public Schools, Washington. Used with permission.

well does the student perform on this standard at the present time?" Finally, each subject area includes its own progress measure that indicates whether the student is learning at a significant, steady, or minimal rate. It's quite possible for a student to be, for instance, meeting expectations at something but growing very slowly, or below expectations but improving rapidly.

Secondary School Examples

Secondary standards-based report cards often maintain the traditional course-based categories (for example, "algebra I"). This makes some organizational sense. In many states, state standards at the high school level are organized into content areas that parallel course offerings (again, like "algebra I.") Another reason that it makes sense to organize secondary report cards by course is that, in an increasing number of states, learning outcomes are measured with end-of-course exams instead of single state tests. Also, the need for a grade-point average exerts some pressure to report course grades.

Secondary school grading reform often focuses not on changing report cards but on making the course grades reflective of achievement. Even if the report card is not changed, high school students, teachers, and parents reap the benefits we already discussed when grades have an interpretable achievement meaning. Students can more easily set meaningful learning goals, teachers can more easily see the results of their teaching, and parents get a better picture of how their children are learning.

Some secondary schools modify their course-based report cards to report participation, effort, homework, or other "learning enabler" grades by subject (Guskey & Bailey, 2010). Figure 5.4 shows how such a report card might be organized.

These standards-based report cards, and others like them, are all set up to be filled with proficiency grades that accurately reflect students' levels of achievement of each of the reporting standards. The following strategies will help to ensure that when you combine grades from individual assessments, the reported proficiency grades will be meaningful.

Strategy 7: Grade on Standards

Langston was a whiz in his high school introductory physics class. He loved the subject, enjoyed reading the textbook, and had an uncanny ability to discern the concepts behind the facts and figures in the various problems the class solved. He was, as his classmates said, "really into it." In Mr. Washington's class, grades were based on tests (50 percent), lab reports and written problems (40 percent), and participation in class (10 percent). Mr. Washington

Course/Teacher		1st Quarter	2nd Quarter	3rd Quarter	4th Quarter	Final Exam	Final Grade
English	**Achievement Grade**						
Mr. Williams	Work Habits/Homework						
	Participation/Collaboration						
	Initiative						
Algebra II	**Achievement Grade**						
Ms. Johnson	Work Habits/Homework						
	Participation/Collaboration						
	Initiative						
Biology	**Achievement Grade**						
Mr. Robinson	Work Habits/Homework						
	Participation/Collaboration						
	Initiative						
World Cultures	**Achievement Grade**						
Ms. Sanchez	Work Habits/Homework						
	Participation/Collaboration						
	Initiative						

Achievement Grades
A 90–100
B 80–89
C 70–79
D 60–69
F Below 60

Work and Study Habits
4 Exceeds expectations
3 Meets expectations
2 Approaches expectations
1 Does not meet expectations

Figure 5.4: Course-based secondary report card with separate marks for achievement and work habits.

used an A, B, C, D, F scale, in which 93–100 percent was an A. Langston aced the tests, reports, and problems but never spoke in class. He was too shy to help others who were stuck, even when he knew how to explain the physics. Langston routinely received final grades of around 92 percent, and his report card grade was often a B. Langston's parents had no idea he was a physics whiz, and the colleges to which he applied couldn't see it, either.

Just as grades for individual assignments should be based on achievement for those assignments (Strategy 5), final grades should be appraisals of achievement for a set of assignments. Accomplish this first by making sure each individual assessment represents achievement of a standard or part of a standard, and second by making sure you combine the achievement grades in such a way that each one's weight in the final grade reflects the portion of standards-based achievement the assessment represented.

What I have called "blueprint thinking" is helpful here. Look at the information contained in the set of assessments for a reporting period. How is information about the different content and skills in the reporting standard balanced? How are various kinds of thinking and reasoning represented in the assessments? The whole (final grade) will be the sum of its parts (individual assignment grades).

Reporting Nonachievement Factors

Figure 1.1 (page 8) showed that even though you don't *grade* effort and other learning enablers, you can report them. How do you do that? The same principles we have been using for standards-based reporting of achievement apply to the reporting of nonachievement factors. Start with defining what nonachievement factors you value. Make them clear and consistent with classroom expectations so that the students get the same message.

Typically, districts want to create their own lists of nonachievement indicators that are appropriate for their specific contexts. Creating such a list is a good opportunity for teacher involvement in policymaking, because these student behaviors occur, are nurtured, and are coached and evaluated in the classroom. Lists of learning and social skills for report cards should have the following characteristics:

- They should focus on important behaviors that generalize across classroom settings (for example, "Keeps work space organized," not "Puts crayons away").

- They should be specific enough to be clear to students (for example, "Cooperates and interacts positively with others," not "Acts nicely").

- They should be differentiated so that indicators are separate and not redundant.

- They should be brief enough to be manageable (a list of priority learning and social skills that educators in the district agree on, not every little thing you might want students to do).

I know of a high school that has four classroom and school rules: be safe; be responsible; be respectful; be a learner. The school works hard at these rules, and they serve as reference points for discussing behavior in classrooms—and sometimes for rewarding and punishing those behaviors. With these as the learning and social skills explicitly valued in the classroom, it would not make sense to use a different set of indicators on the report card. If this school decided to use nonachievement indicators on its report card, it should start with these categories and write a few indicator statements under each one. For example, the "Be a Learner" category might include indicators like "sets and monitors learning goals," "works independently," and so on.

Having separate nonachievement indicators on the report card gives you a way to report the learning skills and behaviors you value without confounding them into the standards-based achievement grades. This approach usually helps teachers who are wary of a transition to standards-based grading, predicting that students will not turn in work promptly, come prepared for class, or show other learning-enabling behaviors unless they "count."

Another important function nonachievement indicators serve is an educative one. First, the indicators themselves make explicit for students what it is that you value in a learner's behavior and give them a target to aim for. And second, you can use the performance on these indicators to help students and parents figure out the reasons for the reported achievement levels, especially less than satisfactory ones, and figure out what to do about it.

For example, a student whose report card lists "basic" on the standard "Computes perimeter, area, and volume" and also "sometimes" for the behavior "Uses class time appropriately" might be led to understand how he could more productively use his class time in mathematics so that he might achieve at a higher level. Paying attention, working persistently, asking for help when needed, and so on, are ways to use class time appropriately that should help him with his geometry. Scores in both domains should rise, but more importantly, the student should become a more self-regulated learner as he makes the connection between classwork and learning.

Choosing Scales for Nonachievement Factors

Standards-based report cards, such as the one shown in figure 5.3 (page 71), typically use a different scale or set of categories for learning and social skills indicators than for academic achievement grades. For example, you might use proficiency categories (*beginning, progressing, proficient, advanced*) for reporting achievement of academic standards and a frequency scale (*consistently, often, sometimes, rarely*) for reporting learning and social skills. Or you might use a 1, 2, 3, 4 scale for reporting achievement of academic standards and a set of letters or other symbols with a separate key for reporting learning and social skills.

Proficiency categories, in my opinion, do *not* make sense as a scale for effort or behavior. What does it mean to be proficient in paying attention, for example? More sensible are lists of learning skills or behaviors with frequency ratings. School districts sometimes use lists of learning skills or behaviors with descriptive evaluations (for example, *outstanding, satisfactory, needs improvement*). This also makes sense, although the frequency scale conveys more information than these evaluative categories.

Frequency scales, which indicate how often a student is observed exhibiting various learning skills, have another important quality. They are "low inference" measures, as opposed to "high inference" measures. Low-inference measures rely on observable behaviors and are more reliable in the sense that different raters would agree. High-inference measures overlay judgment (the "inference") on top of observations. Raters might agree about an observation (for example, that the student *sometimes* turns in homework) and yet disagree about whether that student's homework behavior was satisfactory or needed improvement.

Suppose, for example, that the learning skill "Cooperates and works productively with others" has a more evaluative scale, such as *outstanding, adequate,* and *unsatisfactory.* If a student often works cooperatively, is that outstanding? Or is it merely adequate, doing what's expected? Scales like this require a second judgment beyond how often a skill is observed. And the more subjectivity—the more "play"—in the scale, the less reliable it is.

Even with a frequency scale, most of the learning skills and other important behaviors on such lists are likely to be indicators requiring inferences from some sort of evidence. For example, students don't walk around saying, "I'm showing willingness to try now." You would infer their adaptability from observing their actions. What would you want to observe about a student to decide to what degree he or she "shows willingness to try"? If a student said, "What do I need to do to be better at showing willingness to try?" what would you tell him or her? If a parent said, "Why does my student have a 3 on 'shows willingness to try'?" what would you say?

The answers to these questions identify the *evidence* on which you would base your inferences for each indicator. Seek common agreement on the kinds of evidence needed for each indicator, and then document it. Some districts have a user guide or teacher handbook for their standards-based report cards that lists the kinds of observations that can be evidence for various indicators.

The rubric in figure 5.2 details the evidence teachers would look for to rate students on the indicators used in the Lincoln Public Schools.

Attendance

Attendance is a nonachievement factor with a long history of being valued in schools, and it has obvious measures: numbers of days present and absent. Probably for that reason, it has long been the convention to report, for each reporting period, the number of days a student was absent and tardy, and sometimes the number of days present and/or the total days enrolled. Attendance information is a feature of both standards-based and traditional report cards.

The difference in a standards-based system is that attendance should not be confounded with achievement. In truth, it shouldn't be confounded with achievement in a district that uses traditional grading, either, but sometimes it is. I have known of school districts in which students with more than a certain number of absences in a report period received an automatic *F*. This creates a problem for meaningfully reporting achievement over the year, because the year's average for the subject will include a zero for one-quarter of the year, no matter what the student learned.

Ideally, the grade for a student with a prolonged absence during a quarter should be "not enough information," but that requires that such a possibility exist in the district grading policy. This is easier to accomplish with a standards-based system, in which not all standards are necessarily taught, assessed, and reported in every report period.

Strategy 8: State Grading Policy Clearly

Daniela was a straight-A student at her high school. One of her teachers told her he thought she was on track to be the valedictorian at her high school graduation ceremony. Excited, her parents called family members in other states, and they planned a big family reunion around Daniela's graduation. Imagine their surprise and disappointment when another student was asked to be valedictorian! It turns out that Daniela's classmate had taken a combination of courses that, in the weighted grading system the school used to calculate grade-point averages, put him three-thousandths of a point ahead of Daniela.

The use of grade-point averages is only one of many grading policies that should be explicitly stated. In fact, rules for grade-point averages are one of the few grading policies you can count on being written down somewhere. Many so-called grading policies at the district level are not full policies but just statements of cutoff points on a percentage scale (93–100=A, and so on) and a description of how grade-point averages are calculated. I recommend that grading policies be more complete than that. Districts should spell out what they intend grades to mean and how they intend grades to be used. Figure 5.5 lists issues that district-level grading policies may address and suggests strategies for communicating those policies.

Classroom Policies and District Policies

Thus far in this section, we have been talking about district-level grading policies. Teachers should have classroom-level grading policies, as well. While classroom grading policies should of course be consistent with district-level policy, they are intended to describe for students how you personally will handle the details of grading in your class. For example, figure 3.1 (page 33) showed a

---

Possible Issues to Address in District Grading Policies

- Overall philosophy of using assessment to support learning and description of a balanced assessment system, including both formative and summative assessments

- Intended purpose for grades (for example, describing performance level on standards, providing information for decision making)

- Primary intended audience for grades (for example, school district, parents, students)

- Description of district uses for grades, if appropriate (for example, if used in routine selection or placement decisions)

- Format for reporting (for example, report cards, district website)

- Reporting dates (for example, quarters, trimesters)

- Policy and rationale for separating achievement and nonachievement indicators

- Symbol system and key to its meaning (for example, proficiency scale, letter grades, percentages) for both achievement grades and nonachievement indicators

- Definitions of *passing* or *proficient*

- Policy and rationale for not grading practice work

- Accepted methods of combining evidence for each learning target (for example, using the most recent evidence, using the median)

- Policy for borderline review (gathering additional achievement evidence for students whose grades fall on the border between two grade categories)

- Methods of handling nonsubmission of work

- Methods of handling requests for resubmission of work

Figure 5.5: District grading policy issues and means of communication. continued →

- Policy and rationale for calculating grade-point averages and methods for doing so (for example, weighting for report-period grades and exams); alternatively, policy and rationale for not calculating grade-point averages

Strategies for Communicating District Grading Policies

- Print policies on report card (especially purpose for, audience for, and meaning of grades)
- Create information brochure for parents (to be sent home with report cards)
- Create printed policy document (alone or as part of a student handbook)
- Create Web-based policy document (downloadable)

Typically, these strategies are used in combination. For example, a district's report card might have a boxed purpose statement and a description of the meaning of grading symbols, and a more detailed policy statement available in print and online would include more complete information about all grading issues.

classroom grading policy that was specifically about resubmitting work. Figure 5.6 is an example of a general classroom grading policy. You can use this as a template to which you might add specific policies such as the one in figure 3.1.

The drafting of classroom grading policies is a great opportunity to involve students by soliciting their input. Of course, there are some things that are not negotiable—for example, that the teacher gives the grades and has final say over which individual assessment grades go into the report card grade. But within that framework, students can contribute suggestions on a number of issues—for example, the details of the policy for making up missed work. Sharing these decisions helps engage students and, for most, increases buy-in and feelings of agency and control.

Grading Policy, *[Teacher's Name], [Class, Grade, or Course Name]*

I will use a variety of assessment methods. Formative (practice) assessments will receive feedback and should show students what they need to do for successful performance on graded assessments. For each graded assessment, whether graded with a rubric (as in the case of a paper or project) or with percentage of total points (as in the case of a test), I will designate one of the following proficiency categories:

Advanced means achievement of a standard at a level of performance beyond what is expected. Usually, advanced performance means students have added original insights to their work, made connections to other subjects or texts, or applied their knowledge to a new context beyond the assignment. Students should not expect to be advanced in performance on every standard.

Proficient means achievement of a standard at an expected level of performance. Performance expectations are described for each assignment and are derived from the [state name] performance level descriptors and grade-level expectations.

Nearing proficient means a student's performance is not at the expected level yet, but the quality of the work gives evidence that the student can be, or soon will be, at the expected level of performance on a standard with additional practice. Students who receive a grade of nearing proficient on an assignment may talk with me about additional practice that might help them reach the proficient level.

Novice means a student's performance indicates that the student does not yet have the knowledge and skills defined for a particular standard.

Conclusions about overall performance for each standard on the report card will be based on the body of evidence from assessments of that standard. To evaluate the student's overall achievement for each standard, I will use the median performance level except in unusual cases. In the rare cases where the median does not seem an appropriate evaluation of performance, I will provide a narrative explanation with the report card.

Students or parents who have questions about grades should ask me for a conference. If a student demonstrates achievement at the novice level for many standards, or over time, I may ask the student to work under a grading contract and/or use modified assignments.

Figure 5.6: General classroom grading policy.

Reasons for Documenting Policies

I recommend that classroom teachers document their classroom grading policies with a formal statement such as the one in figure 5.6 and that districts document their school district policies in one of the ways suggested in figure 5.5. And I strongly recommend that they discuss the intended meanings and uses of the grades with students and parents. These recommendations are in keeping with our second principle, that grading policies should support and motivate student effort and learning. Students need to know your grading policy if they are to work within it. In a standards-based system, grading policies in effect become statements of how you are going to report students' learning. Clear grading policies will also contribute, at least among older students, to perceptions of fairness in grading, which will in turn contribute to students' motivation.

There is also a legal reason for documenting grading policies. Grades can be, and have been, challenged in court. Almost always, the legal principle under which students and parents have challenged students' grades is either the due-process provision or the equal-protection provision of the Fourteenth Amendment to the U.S. Constitution (McElligott & Brookhart, 2009). In the event of a challenge, a written grading policy will give evidence of what process you intended to use. Students and parents need to be aware of what the process is in order to see whether they have been duly treated according to the policy.

Strategy 9: Keep Standards-Based Records

Ms. Fisher was very excited about her district's new standards-based report cards. She knew she already practiced standards-based instruction. The sixth-grade team had done a lot of "unpacking standards" exercises, and she was sure that her instruction did indeed represent the knowledge and skills in her state standards. She didn't really change the way she recorded her grades, however, because it was so easy to use the same gradebook software she had always used.

At the end of the first quarter, she realized she had a set of grades for each of the subjects (for example, reading and mathematics) but not for the itemized standards under the subjects (for example, vocabulary, fluency, number sense, measurement, and geometry). Oh, well, she reasoned, if a student is proficient in reading, he or she must be proficient in vocabulary and fluency. Thus, her grades for all the standards in each subject area were the same.

The problem with this approach, as most readers have already figured out, is that if every student has the same grade for each of the standards in a subject area, the standards-based report card communicates no more information than a conventional subject-matter list. All those standards are sort of a waste of space, as far as communication about student performance is concerned, if they're all based on the same evidence. It is certainly possible—and even likely—that some students will have the same grade (for example, proficient) in every standard in a subject area, but many will have different grades. Identifying strengths and weaknesses by standard is part of the reason for having the more detailed report card.

What Evidence Should Be Recorded?

In the gradebook from which you will figure final grades, record students' grades for final, summative work. Formative assessments should not figure into grades. While some formative assessments are informal and don't lead to scores or symbols, others—like quizzes and class exercises—yield data that look a lot like what teachers have been used to recording as grades. Be careful not to confuse formative assessment evidence with the ingredients for grades.

It is often helpful to record information from the more formal formative assessments, but the purpose for doing so is instructional. Some school districts, like the Spokane Public Schools, support this approach with a grade-book program designed to include both formative and summative assessment results. Some classroom teachers enter only summative assessments (grading ingredients) into their gradebook software and have students keep track of their formative assessments. Some gradebook software allows you to enter formative information but give it a weight of zero for calculating the final grade.

How Much Evidence Should Be Recorded?

Teachers sometimes ask, "How many individual grades should I record for each standard?" For teachers who were used to grading "everything"—often having a grade on something for every day—a set of grades for one standard might look small. Other things being equal, more evidence does give stronger support for the final grading decision, but only up to a point.

Get enough evidence, but not too much. Get enough evidence to be confident that your assessments have sampled quite a bit of the domain of learning defined by the standard. But don't get too much evidence. Additional "grades" from assessments that were for practice or from assessments that did not match the intended standard will only muddy the waters and may lead to invalid grading decisions.

In What Form Should Evidence Be Recorded?

The simplest and, in most contexts, best way to do standards-based grading is to record individual grades using scales keyed to the same performance standards that will be used to report academic achievement on the report card. That could be 1, 2, 3, 4; or *novice, nearing proficiency, proficient, advanced*; or even *A, B, C, D, F* for a more traditional report card.

Convert the results of all assessments, no matter what form they start out in, to the performance scale. For tests and other percentage-graded assessments, you will need cut scores. These cut scores *need not be the same for each assessment*, as they are in traditional grading. The cut scores will vary because different assessments require different proficiencies. The key is to get performance to match the proficiency description in the grading scale. So for example, performance on a test that includes many advanced-level questions might have lower cut scores for advanced and proficient than performance on a simple test checking knowledge of key vocabulary terms.

Recording grades on the performance scale used on the report card makes the results of assessments with noncomparable scales—such as tests that yield percentages and performance assessments that yield rubric ratings—comparable. This makes it much easier to maintain standards-based meaning when blending evidence (see Strategy 11). For years, a source of invalidity in grades has been teachers' practice of blending evidence by averaging scores on non-comparable scales without realizing that the grades that resulted from their calculations did not, in fact, mean what they intended (Brookhart, 1999a).

How Should Evidence Be Recorded?

Recording evidence for grading by standard requires different recording formats from traditional grading. Figure 5.7 shows one method of record keeping by standard (in this case the reading standards from the report card in figure 5.3, page 71) that requires a separate page for each student. It is useful for elementary teachers who have one class. A page per student is not efficient for teachers with a large number of students. Figure 5.8 shows an example of a record-keeping form that can be used for a group of students. This one is more useful in secondary schools.

Student _____ Quarter/Year _____												
Evidence												
Standard	11/19 Portfolio	11/23 Drawing	12/1 Portfolio	12/7 Oral	12/10 Tests	12/13 Portfolio	12/15 Essays	1/5 Portfolio	1/10 Oral	1/13 Tests	1/19 Portfolio	1/24 Essays	Summary
Understands and uses different skills and strategies to read	2		2		2	2	2	3		3	3	3	3
Understands the meaning of what is read	2	2	1	2	1	2	2	3	3	3	3	3	3
Reads different materials for a variety of purposes	3		2			2		2			2		2
Sets goals and evaluates progress to improve reading	3		3			3		3			3		3
Comments													

Figure 5.7: Summarizing evidence for one student.

Most schools use some form of electronic record keeping. Gradebook software can reduce the burden of standards-based record keeping because one of the things computers do well is store and organize data. Some school districts contract with a programmer to develop software when they develop new report cards. Many commercially available gradebook programs can be set up to accommodate the standards-based grading practices recommended in this book.

It is critical when using any gradebook program to have someone examine the default settings and make sure they are reset to accommodate standards-based grading in general and your class and district grading policies in particular. For example, what kind of "averaging" is done? If you plan to use the

Student	Standard #1						Standard #2						Standard #3						Add sections for standards and assessments as needed.	Summary		
	*	*	*	*	*	*	*	*	*	*	*	*	*	*	*	*	*	*		St.1	St.2	St.3
A																						
B																						
C																						
D																						
E																						
F																						
G																						
H																						
I																						
J																						
K																						
L																						
M																						
N																						
O																						
P																						
Q																						
R																						
S																						
etc.																						

*Fill in dates and/or assessment names here, grouped under the standard for which they are indicators. List standard names in row 1 (replacing "Standard #1," "Standard #2," and so on). Record proficiency levels (such as 1, 2, 3, 4) in cells, in rows according to students' names.

Figure 5.8: Summarizing evidence for a group of students.

median (see Strategy 11) but the default setting is to use the mean, you need to know that and change the setting.

The following questions suggest things to look for in gradebook software:

- Is there a method (perhaps separate pages by category or a coding system) to record individual grades for each standard separately?

- What kind of averaging or summarizing does the program do to combine individual grades? Can you set it to use the method you intend to use? Is there an override option for special cases, when for some reason calculated final grades do not represent a student's current achievement status accurately?

- What kind of weighting of individual assignments does the program do? Can the weights be specified?

Strategy 10: Use Multiple Measures

Ms. Coleman was working on a grade 9–10 core standard in writing: "Write arguments to support claims in an analysis of substantive topics or texts, using valid reasoning and relevant and sufficient evidence." The class had talked about stating and supporting a thesis or an argument and had read lots of examples of this kind of writing. Ms. Coleman had given several graded writing assessments during the quarter. Two had been response-to-literature pieces based on stories the students had read and discussed. One had been an assignment to write a letter to the editor of the school newspaper.

Madison had lots of opinions. In fact, she had an opinion about almost everything. She was not shy about stating and supporting her point of view. She enjoyed writing and used language well. All three of her writing assessments for this standard were rated advanced.

Destiny, however, struggled. Reading skills were not her strongest suit, and she had more difficulty with the response-to-literature pieces than Madison did. Her work was right on the border between proficient and nearing proficient. After the second assessment, Ms. Coleman was still wondering which grade Destiny should get for the quarter.

Destiny was on the student council and worked in a program that assigned students to provide various services around the school. Destiny picked up a lot of litter, and she had lots of experience-based knowledge about who littered, and why, and what might be done about it. She wrote a simple but eloquent letter to the editor of the school newspaper, titled "Help Fight Litter," with a clear thesis statement and lots of reasons and evidence. That piece was truly proficient. It showed Ms. Coleman that when Destiny had a good grasp of the topic, she was able to take a position and support it with reasoning and evidence in an organized, logical, and well-written piece. This was the information Ms. Coleman needed to be confident that Destiny's performance on this standard was proficient.

Of course, using multiple measures does not make all students proficient. It is actually quite common that students' performance on a set of multiple measures on the same construct is consistent—sometimes consistently not proficient. In that case, the multiple measures just give you more confidence that the judgment of nonproficiency is accurate. But sometimes, as in this scenario, you get additional information about what students can do.

Reasons to Use Multiple Measures in Grading

There are several reasons to use multiple measures for standards-based grading. We'll consider two of the most important ones here. First, consider that most standards are complex—that is, they define a domain that encompasses a variety of related knowledge and skills. If the grade is to convey meaningful information about a student's proficiency in that domain, using multiple, complementary measures helps ensure representation of more of the domain than one measure alone. The set of items or tasks on any one test or performance assessment cannot adequately represent the depth and breadth of a complex construct such as "Understands and uses different skills and strategies to read." Several measures, taken together, give a more representative picture of the depth and breadth of student performance in this domain. In this example, evidence might come from multiple observations of students' oral reading of different stories and materials, a student reflection in a reading portfolio, and a reading comprehension test that focused on strategy use.

A second reason for using multiple measures is that all measurement includes error. "Error" in this sense doesn't mean that you or the student did anything wrong. It means that any one score or grade is an imperfect estimate of a student's true performance. You sometimes hear teachers refer to this fact when they say that a student "had a bad day." Actually, it's also possible that a student can "have a good day" and get a grade that overrepresents performance. (Did you ever get back a test on which several lucky guesses made your work look better than it really was?) Student performance can vary with the assessment format or context, as for example when a student who never played baseball doesn't have the background knowledge that other students might, and it interferes with comprehension of a story about baseball.

If you do not have enough individual grades to make a valid grading decision for a particular standard, it is better not to give a grade on that standard for that quarter or report period. In fact, one of the good things about standards-based report cards is that most of them do offer the option of not giving a grade for a standard, which is not the case in traditional grading. Plan ahead to make sure you have enough evidence for all of the standards you should be grading for any given report period.

Strategy 11: Maintain Standards-Based Meaning When Blending Evidence

Tiara and Tatiana were twins. They were each in a different section of high school biology, but both sections were using the same curriculum framework and common departmental unit tests. Mr. Smith, Tiara's teacher, also used labs that were assessed by individual worksheets. Students did labs in pairs and then were individually assessed on a set of questions and tasks that included recall of facts, explanation of what happened during the lab and what they learned from it (which required reasoning from both the lab results and other information from the unit), and sometimes drawings. Mr. Smith also added into his grade a participation component, which included things like coming prepared for class, doing homework, and participating in class discussions. He averaged test scores (weighted as one-third of the final grade), lab worksheets (one-third), and participation (one-third) to arrive at his final grades for each quarter.

Mr. Jones, Tatiana's teacher, used the common departmental unit tests and labs, too. For his labs, students were required to write conventional lab reports (with introduction, method, results, and conclusions sections). He also had students do independent investigations on topics of their choice (related to the standards they were studying, of course) and write reports or make presentations about them. He averaged test scores (weighted as 40 percent of the final grade), lab reports (40 percent), and independent investigations (20 percent) to arrive at his final grades for each quarter.

Tiara and Tatiana emerged from their first quarter with about the same amount of knowledge and skills on the biology standards they were responsible for during that time. Tiara's grade was a B. Her test scores and lab worksheet were in the B– to C– range, and her participation was an A. Tatiana's grade was a C. Like her sister, her test scores and lab reports were in the B– to C– range. Her independent investigation for that quarter was a B.

Mr. Jones had the standards-based evidence (from tests, labs, and the independent investigation) to know that Tatiana's biology achievement was a C. Mr. Smith mixed in a heavily weighted (one-third of the grade) participation factor for Tiara, and her biology grade of *B* did not maintain the standards-based meaning.

Weighting Considerations

Assuming that you have kept standards-based records (Strategy 9) and that you have several records per standard (Strategy 10), for each student you will have a body of evidence that comprises that student's performance in regard to that standard. The object is to evaluate the body of evidence—all the work together—in such a way that you accurately describe the student's achievement regarding that standard. You will have separately recorded participation and other effort and behavior indicators to report in a learning and social skills scale, so these will have no weight in the academic achievement grades.

How should you decide what weight to give to different pieces of achievement evidence, those different grades from individual assessments? Use the following factors to decide on the relative weight individual assessment grades should have in the final report card grade.

- **Importance of content knowledge and skills in relation to standards.** Student performance on content knowledge and skills that are integral to the standard should carry more weight than performance on less important content knowledge and skills. Your own discipline-specific knowledge and deep understanding of the standards are crucial here.

- **Importance of content knowledge and skills in light of instruction.** Students will expect content knowledge and skills you (and they) spent more time on, or which you emphasized in class, to be weighted more heavily in their grade. Of course, this comes with a corollary recommendation: spend more instructional time on and give more emphasis to important content knowledge and skills.

- **Recency of evidence.** The term *achievement* implies a learning process. Students progress from less able to more able on a particular standard. Their report cards should reflect their current status or accomplishments. Thus, if there are several grades for a similar aspect of a standard, the more recent ones should carry more weight in the final grade.

- **Performance patterns.** When you evaluate a body of evidence, you have the opportunity to look at student performance over time. When there are several grades for a similar aspect of a standard, you can evaluate performance patterns—for example, gradual improvement, gradual decline, consistency, or erratic performance. Sometimes figuring out the reasons for these patterns will also give you clues about student achievement.

Evaluating a Body of Evidence for a Final Grade

Once you have made decisions about what evidence is more important and should carry more weight in the final grade, and what evidence is less important and should carry less weight, you are ready to combine the individual assessment grades (the components or "ingredients") into a report card grade.

A conventional way to do this in traditional grading has been to record grades in percentages and then average. Weighting is then a matter of multiplying each set of scores (each column in the gradebook) by its intended weight, and then taking the mean of the weighted scores for each student's grade. Because I'm recommending a change from conventional grading practices, I won't illustrate that here. You can see an example of weighted averaging in my later illustration of the devastating effect of zeros (fig. 5.9, page 95).

While I don't recommend weighted averaging for most K–12 grading purposes, it might be appropriate in some college contexts. For example, in a survey course on Renaissance history in which students take a series of tests, each representing a different set of topics, and then receive one final course grade, it makes sense to average the test scores measured as percentages. This is not the case in most K–12 contexts.

Reasons Not to Use the Mean to Summarize Evidence

The *mean* is the arithmetic average, which is what most people are referring to when they use the word *average*. Actually, there are many kinds of averages, and the mean is just one of them.

One reason for not recommending using the mean or weighted mean is the disproportionate effects of extreme scores like zeros. Another reason is that averaging across a whole report period does a disservice to the concept of learning, which is about growing and changing. If a student didn't write very well at the beginning of the year but has improved by the end of the grading period, that student should not still be saddled with the effects of a low grade, which will pull down the achievement level reported. A third reason has to do with number properties. Grades that are recorded in standards-based terms (*advanced, proficient,* and so on), *even if numbers are used for the levels* (4, 3, 2, 1, for example), do *not* provide the kind of numbers for which a mean can be meaningfully calculated. Proficiency-level categories are ordinal. That is, they only tell order (*advanced* is higher than *proficient,* and so on). They don't measure "inches of learning" as rulers measure inches of length.

It won't surprise the mathematics teachers who are reading this, but it might surprise some other readers to hear that there are other kinds of "averages" besides the mean. I think that the best method for combining a set of individual grades into a report card grade for most standards-based grading contexts is to use the median.

Reasons for Using the Median to Summarize Evidence

If you can put numbers in order, you can use the median to describe typical performance. The median is one kind of average—it's the fiftieth percentile. Half of the scores in a group are above the median, and half are below. The median doesn't require that your grades be composed of equal-interval steps, or even that they be numbers. To use a median, grades only have to be on some scale that is ordered from low to high. So if each individual assessment has been judged *beginning, progressing, proficient,* and *advanced,* for instance, that's enough. Those are ordered categories.

I'm going to show you how to calculate a median so that you can understand the concept. In reality, you would not calculate the median by hand. You would set your gradebook or spreadsheet to do it. But once you see how easy it is, the median may make more sense to you.

Let's look at an example. Figure 5.7 (page 84) presented a summary sheet that a teacher might use for the reading section of the report card in figure 5.3 (page 71). On each of the dates listed, the teacher administered an assessment of some sort. For each of the assessments, the teacher assigned a grade in the comprehension category ("Understands the meaning of what is read"). Some of the assessments also included tasks that allowed the teacher to assess students' understanding and use of different reading strategies, their skill at reading for a variety of purposes, and their ability to set goals to improve reading. Notice that not every cell was filled. In other examples—in other subjects, for instance—there might be even more of a checkerboard pattern, as some assessments address one or two standards and not others.

To learn how to calculate the median, look at the grades for "Reads different materials for a variety of purposes":

3   2   2   2   2

First, line the grades up in order, from smaller to larger; then count to the middle score:

2   2   ②   2   3

The median is 2. In this simple example, where the scores on the summary sheet were already in order from larger to smaller, it might not seem to make a difference. I advise you to get used to doing it this way, though, because not all sets of grades will be this simple.

In an even-numbered set of scores, the median will be between two grades. If the median is between two grades that are the same (two 2s, or two 3s, for example), then the median is that grade. If the median is between two grades that are not the same, the median is the number or category halfway between them.

Traditional grading may give you the option of using "between" grades, for instance *A–* or *B+*. In a standards-based system, where the numbers represent categories, there is no "between" category. So, for example, if the median is between a 2 and a 3, as in the following series of scores, you have a borderline grade:

   2   2   2⟨ ⟩3   3   3

Use additional achievement information (not effort or behavior) to decide which category is the best summary of the student's current achievement status. We'll have more to say about borderline grades later in this section.

For a mathematician, the argument that the median is the proper summary statistic or "average" to use with ordinal data like grades is sufficient to justify its use. I know, however, that some readers have been doing the more familiar kind of "averaging" (using the mean) for so long that the median may still feel strange. For those readers, I hope the following illustration of the way the median works helps to convince you that changing your method from mean to median is worthwhile.

The median does not give extra weight to extreme scores the way the mean does. A very low score is just another score in the bottom half, and a very high score is just another score in the upper half. Do you remember ever having a teacher who let you "drop" your lowest grade so that the average was not "pulled down"? That was a concession to the fact that extreme scores affect means. But it was also contrary to the concept that the grade is supposed to reflect achievement. Maybe you achieved an *F*, but it didn't count because the teacher was trying to be kind. So what was being graded—some combination of student achievement and teacher kindness?

Using the median avoids all that. It lets you actually use all the evidence (including that low grade) and yet not have the final grade be unduly pulled by any extreme. Here is an example using standards-based categories (*beginning, progressing, proficient, advanced*), represented here by 1, 2, 3, 4:

   1   2   2   3   3   3   3

You would *not* take the mean of this set of grades—they're not that kind of number. For the sake of illustration, though, it's worth pointing out that the mean would be a 2 (2.43), not a 3. Using the median, the student's report card grade is a 3 and *legitimately does* reflect that one low grade. Again, for nonmathematicians who may see this as some sort of trick—it's not. Three is really the fiftieth percentile of this set of grades and really represents typical performance in that sense.

Here is an example, using the traditional A, B, C, D, F scale, in which one low grade is kept but does not unduly influence an average:

F   D   C   B   B   B   A

You would *not* take the mean of this set of grades, either—although in a traditional context, people do. Using the traditional point system (F = Ø through A=4), the mean of this set of grades would also be 2.43, a C or maybe a C+. The median, however, would be a B.

My bottom line is this: if you are going to average grades, the median is the average to use, as opposed to the mean (or the mode, or any of the other mathematical "averages"). Calculating the median and then reviewing it, using judgment informed by both median performance and patterns of performance, including recency of evidence, will lead to even more accurate communication about student achievement. The next section discusses judgment-based use of recency of evidence.

Emphasizing Recent Evidence

If report card grades are to communicate the status of students' achievement, they should reflect what the student can do at the time the report card is issued. To accomplish this purpose, you need to take into account the recency of the evidence and whether there was a pattern of growth (or decline) on a standard over time.

For our illustration of how to consider recency of evidence, look at the individual grades for "Understands the meaning of what is read" in figure 5.7, ordered from smallest to largest:

1   1   2   2   2   2   2   2   3   3   3   3

The median is 2. But is 2 (approaching performance expectations) a true indicator of the student's current status in comprehension?

Look at the pattern when the grades are ordered by date:

2   2   1   2   1   2   2   3   3   3   2   3

The student started out the quarter pretty reliably at a 2 level (approaching performance expectations) and ended the quarter pretty reliably at a 3 level (meeting performance expectations). This was not a fluke. It was not one 3 or 4 at the end of a long line of 2s. It was a discernible pattern.

For a pattern such as this, I recommend that judgment take precedence over the strict calculation of the median. In this case, I would assign the student a 3 for "Understands the meaning of what is read" even if it meant manually overriding the gradebook software that calculated the median of 2. Following the same reasoning, the grade for "Understands and uses different strategies to read" is also a 3, although the median is 2.

Note that the recency principle doesn't work for traditional grading. Grades from assessments early in the report period might be about something different than later grades. In a middle school general science class, a student might not understand cell division but ace photosynthesis, for example. That's not growth so much as different performance on different standards. So the recommendation to consider recency of evidence is conditional. Weight more recent evidence more heavily than older evidence only if you are working with a set of individual grades that all assess the same standard.

Distinguishing Failure From Failure to Try

Concern about the need to distinguish failure from failure to try arose in the context of traditional grading. People began to think about the disproportionate effect of zeros—often the grade assigned if students fail to turn in work—on the mean or average of a set of percentage grades. As Reeves (2004) and others have noted, this is a matter of mathematical logic and is really not up for debate. The "zero problem" is an artifact of the percentage scale. In the percentage scale, the *F* range is very large compared with the range for the other grades. Therefore, a "low F" (any very low *F*, really, not just a zero) has a disproportionate pull on the mean compared with a "low D" or "low C," for example.

Figure 5.9 gives data for four different "what-if" scenarios featuring Derrick, a student in a traditionally graded class. In the top panel, the scenarios are played out in a system that uses percentages as assignment grades. In the bottom panel, the same scenarios are played out in a system that uses letter grades for assignments. The top panel demonstrates how the unbalanced grade ranges in the percentage scale are the reason for the disproportionate effect of zero. The bottom panel shows that this effect disappears when unequal grade ranges disappear.

The first row of each panel shows that when you average Derrick's performance on all the assessments for the report period, his overall achievement is about at the *C* level—although whether he would remain a *C* student in a standards-based context is questionable. It depends on whether the test, quizzes, paper, and project all measured the same standard, which they may not have done, and whether all of the assessments were given after Derrick truly had a chance to learn and practice.

The four scenarios illustrate the effect in a traditional grading context of using a zero to mean failure to try. Derrick receives the same grades for his

A. The effect of zero when the percentage (0–100) scale is used

Student	Test (counts double)	Quiz 1	Quiz 2	Paper (counts double)	Project	Report Card Grade
1. Derrick (C on paper)	78%	82%	64%	76%	96%	79% C
2. Derrick (high F on paper)	78%	82%	64%	58%	96%	73% C
3. Derrick (low F on paper)	78%	82%	64%	30%	96%	65% D
4. Derrick (zero on paper)	78%	82%	64%	0%	96%	57% F

B. The effect of zero when the A=4, B=3, C=2, D=1, F=0 scale is used

Student	Test (counts double)	Quiz 1	Quiz 2	Paper (counts double)	Project	Report Card Grade
1. Derrick (C on paper)	C (2)	B (3)	D (1)	C (2)	A (4)	C+ (2.28)
2. Derrick (high F on paper)	C (2)	B (3)	D (1)	F (0)	A (4)	C– (1.71)
3. Derrick (low F on paper)	C (2)	B (3)	D (1)	F (0)	A (4)	C– (1.71)
4. Derrick (zero on paper)	C (2)	B (3)	D (1)	F (0)	A (4)	C– (1.71)

Figure 5.9: Illustration of the effect of zeros on report card grades.

test, quizzes, and project in all four scenarios, but different grades for his paper in each one. Let's think about Derrick's report card grade for each scenario in the top panel of figure 5.9.

1. What if Derrick's paper had been at about the same level of quality (a *C*) as much of his other work? The first row shows that his final grade, calculated as a weighted average with the test and the paper counting double, would be a *C*.

2. Derrick hates writing papers, and it's really not one of his strengths. What if Derrick's paper had been a high *F*—that is, in the upper range of the huge 0–59 range that represents an *F* in this system? The second row shows that his final grade would still be a *C*.

3. Derrick hates writing papers, and he only does part of the assignment. What if Derrick's paper had been a low *F*—at 30, about halfway down the range that represents an *F*? The third row shows that his final grade would be a *D*.

4. Derrick knows he isn't good at writing papers, and if he turns in a paper it will be a bad one. Dejected, he figures, "Why bother?" What if Derrick didn't turn in the paper, and so was assigned a zero? The fourth row shows that his final grade would be an *F*. That is, the grade for this one paper would define his report card grade, despite the fact that his tested performance was a *C*, the average of his quizzes was a *C*, and his project grade was an *A*.

    4a. Or, try another version of scenario 4. Derrick hates writing papers, is belligerent toward his teacher when the paper is assigned, crosses his arms and declares, "I'm not doin' it." What if Derrick didn't turn in the paper, and so was assigned a zero? The result of this scenario is the same as for the previous version. His final grade would be an *F*.

My point in giving two versions of the fourth scenario is to show that, beyond the devastating effect of zeros on percentage-based averages, there is more going on in failure-to-try situations. In a standards-based grading system, grades are based on achievement, and behavioral issues are handled behaviorally (Strategy 5). So while the numbers worked out the same for Unconfident Derrick and Belligerent Derrick, in standards-based grading the two Derricks would be treated differently.

There are many options for helping Derrick, each requiring that the teacher know something about the student and work with him directly. Remember the assessment information that was for classroom use but not for grading? Here's a time when it will come in handy. Does Derrick truly believe he can't do the paper, and is that belief well founded or not? Is Derrick belligerent in general, or does his attitude have something to do with the paper specifically? Does Derrick have a desk at home where he can actually write?

If Derrick is unable to do the paper as assigned, he might need a modified assignment, one that is simplified or shortened, for example. Or perhaps he can't do such a large project but could do a paper once it was chunked up for him into steps (read about the topic, write a thesis sentence, write an outline, draft the first section, and so on). Would a contract help? How about a quiet workspace at school?

Once you start thinking about failure to try as a behavioral issue, there is not just one solution (give a zero). There are multiple solutions, depending on what the real problem is. And—for me this is the best part—handling the problem behaviorally allows you to work with Derrick. When a teacher gives a zero, that's it—the *teacher* gives the zero. In a behavioral approach, the teacher works *with* the student, which is more consistent with how students learn. When the teacher works with the student, the student retains some control over the situation and may feel like he or she actually has a chance of doing better. Remember, control over one's circumstances is a strong motivator.

Review Borderline Grades

If the purpose of a grade is to communicate student achievement of a standard, what do you do when a student falls between two achievement categories? Suppose, for example, that you are a fourth-grade mathematics teacher using the report card in figure 5.3 (page 71). One of your standards reads:

> **Concept of Area:** Develops an understanding of the spatial relationships of area and perimeter. Solves problems involving perimeter and area of rectangles.

Paige, one of your students, has received the following six grades (on the 1–4 scale, where 3 means "meets expectations at this time"):

2   3   3   2   2   3

The median is between 2 and 3, and you have to decide whether Paige meets performance expectations for concept of area or is approaching performance expectations. The evidence is equivocal. There is no clear pattern (for example, 2, 2, 2, 3, 3, 3 or 3, 3, 3, 2, 2, 2), that would allow the more recent evidence to be interpreted as growth (or decline) in learning. There is just a mixture of 2s and 3s. Further, let's assume that there was no other pattern apparent, for example, if the 2s had all been for tests and the 3s for performance assessments.

What to do? First, avoid the temptation to let nonachievement evidence slip in here. For example, if Paige had been trying very hard, don't be tempted to assign her a grade of 3—meets performance expectations for Concept of Area—for that reason. Instead, look for *additional achievement* evidence. What information do you have about Paige's work on the concept of area besides the six graded assessments? You might have some information from formative (practice) assessments that would help you decide whether she really did have an acceptable concept of area or not. You might have some information from observations or conversations you had with Paige as she did her work. You might have some information from the questions she asked in class.

Let me be very clear here. I'm not suggesting you "grade" these additional pieces of achievement evidence, which were not meant to be graded in the first place, and take the median or do any other calculations. I am suggesting you consider the situation as a question: "Paige's grade is on the border. Which side (2 or 3) is the best description of what I know about her performance on the standard Concept of Area?" Then look at the other achievement evidence you have from Paige. Which side of the fence does that evidence suggest she should fall on? (Because "on the fence" is not one of your choices.) This situation calls for a judgment. Your evaluation should be the grade that you think you can make the best case for, using all the achievement information you have.

Incidentally, reviewing borderline grades in a traditional grading context is also best handled by using additional achievement evidence. For example, if a student's average is 89.5 in a context where 80–89 is a *B* and 90–100 is an *A*, you should use additional achievement evidence to support a judgment. Your evaluation (that the student should receive a *B* or an *A*) should still be the grade that you think you can make the best case for, using all the achievement information you have.

Strategy 12: Involve Students

Cody was in a third-grade class that was working on the operations and algebraic thinking standard "Represent and solve problems involving multiplication and division." For each learning objective under this standard, Ms. Prentiss used informal formative assessments as well as some formal quizzes and other assessments that were intended to be formative (for practice). When Ms. Prentiss intended a particular test to yield one of the grades that she would use in figuring the report card grade, she gave the students enough notice that they could study for the test.

Ms. Prentiss asked the students to keep individual charts of their progress on both formative and summative assessments, in the form of a line graph. She told them to look for a "sawtooth" pattern, in which the formative assessments *leading up to a grade showed increases, and the graded assessment was the peak for that particular skill. Cody saw this pattern most of the time, and it helped him learn that his grades were based on his best performance and that his practice work contributed to that best work. Ms. Prentiss instructed other students, who didn't see this pattern in their work, to conference with her so she could plan how to differentiate instruction, and they could plan how to adjust their study and work habits.*

The teacher in this scenario did several things to involve students. First, she had them keep track of their own performance. Not only did they have a graph of their progress to look at, they had made the graphs themselves. Second, she involved students in interpreting the patterns in their work and especially helped them interpret the relationship of formative practice work (effort) to ultimate achievement. Third, when there was a problem to resolve, she used conferences to include the student in decisions about what to do to address it.

Figure 5.10 summarizes ways teachers can (and do) involve students in grading. Two of my favorites—because they seem particularly powerful—are (1) engage students in establishing grading policies and (2) engage students in tracking their own learning progress.

Use the following strategies to involve students in grading:

- Have students track their own grades on individual assignments over a report period and use the chart or graph to monitor and plan their own study and work.

- Give students input into negotiable aspects of your classroom report card grading policy (for example, policies about makeup work or timelines).

- Use contracts that specify performances required for different levels of achievement (a strategy for some individual students who need a lot of structure).

- Use student goal setting. (Note: Student goal setting should never result in just a goal to "get" a certain grade. Student goal setting should include students' description of what knowledge and skill achievements they are setting as their goals.)

- Have students grade themselves on selected assessments (especially long-term projects and other performance assessments) using the same rubric you do. Then conference with students about your agreement or disagreement with their grades and the reasons for it.

- Use student-led conferences in which students explain to their parents how their report card grades reflect their achievements. Students may give live demonstrations of some of their skills during the conference or may show work they have selected and saved for this occasion (often in a portfolio).

Figure 5.10: Ways to involve students in grading.

Summary

This chapter has described six strategies for grading for report cards:

   7. Grade on standards.

   8. State grading policy clearly.

   9. Keep standards-based records.

   10. Use multiple measures.

   11. Maintain standards-based meaning when blending evidence.

   12. Involve students.

These strategies are best used in a standards-based, or at least learning-focused, reporting system. If grades are assigned by subject (reading, mathematics, and so on), they still are more meaningful and useful if they reflect achievement. Combine grades from individual assignments to reflect achievement of standards-based learning goals within subject areas.

To practice "standards-based" grading in a traditional grading context, almost all of the recommendations in this chapter and the previous chapter still apply. There are two exceptions:

   1. As noted earlier, the recency principle that says more recent evidence should weigh more heavily does not work with a set of grades that represent a mixture of different standards.

   2. Logically, in a traditional grading context, you do not need to keep records sorted according to standard.

In a traditional grading context, using the other ten strategies will *still make for more meaningful grades*, even if those grades are on the old *A, B, C, D, F* scale or are percentages.

Part 3

REFORMING GRADING POLICIES AND PRACTICES TO SUPPORT STUDENT LEARNING

Chapter 6

Beginning and Implementing Learning-Focused Report Card Grading Policies

I hope I have convinced you that grading helps keep the promise of learning for all students if (1) grades reflect student achievement of intended learning outcomes and (2) grading policies support and motivate student effort and learning. I also hope you see how the twelve strategies for grading individual assessments (Strategies 1 to 6) and combining them for report card grades (Strategies 7 to 12) accomplish these goals. If you are interested in this kind of grading, you probably want to know how districts implement learning-focused report card grading policies.

The special focus of this chapter is communication among the educators in the district as policies change and new, standards-based policies are implemented. There must be a means for everyone to know what the new policies are and how to implement them. Teachers and administrators need to work for consistency among themselves so that they are "singing off the same page." Then, of course, they will need to communicate about the new grading policies with students and parents, and that is the focus of chapter 7.

No D, No Zero, and Other Scale-Based Policies

Before we explore strategies that you and your district can use to implement standards-based grading, let's spend a little time looking at some policy changes involving grading scales—the kind that often get into the local newspaper—that miss the mark. How does this happen? It happens when districts start out by discussing the operational details of grading instead of discussing the *purpose* of grading first and allowing decisions to follow from that. Tweaking the scale of grades that are still given for compliance does not turn them into grades that indicate learning.

When I work with teachers around the twelve practical strategies detailed in chapters 4 and 5, I warn them that their colleagues may be opposed to one or another of the strategies and that heated debates seldom advance the cause of grading to support student learning. For example, teachers often vehemently disagree with a no-zero policy in percentage-based grading (Cox & Olsen, 2009). Yet the real issue resides in the underlying assumptions. Teachers who strongly disagree with a no-zero policy also usually believe that grades are the pay students earn for doing what they are asked, and they believe that "responsibility" in that sense should be part of the grade. Teachers who want a no-zero policy usually believe that grades should reflect achievement of academic standards. That is the real disagreement, and those are the grounds for discussion. Without resolving that disagreement, resolving a zero-policy question either won't happen or will result in some compromise that does justice to neither position.

Without a discussion of what grades are supposed to mean—all the issues we discussed in chapter 1—it is quite possible to end up with meaningless policies. I once did a workshop in a district that had already decided there would be a no-zero policy. Because the district administrators had made the decision, they applied this policy to the *report card*, which clearly fell under their jurisdiction. The policy stated that teachers were not allowed to turn in zero grades for report card grades and that the lowest allowed grade was a 59. The district administrators were quite proud of themselves for getting on the "no-zero" bandwagon.

If you think about the case presented in chapter 5 for not assigning zeros in a percentage-based grading system, you will quickly realize that the no-zero recommendation should be implemented at the level of individual assessments, within classrooms. It's a zero grade on an individual assessment, pulling down the average that becomes the report card grade, that makes the report card grade an inaccurate reflection of student achievement.

Under this district's policy, a student could have gotten a zero for not turning in an individual assignment, and it could have pulled down his average so that the teacher turned in, say, a 70 for his report card grade instead of the 80 that more accurately represented his learning. But 70 is not a zero, so the policy is honored—and the damage is done.

What were these district administrators thinking? While I wasn't part of the process, I think it's a safe bet that this misguided district had its discussions at the level of policy details and did not tackle the big question of what the purpose of grading was supposed to be. Now, perhaps, some people in the district think they are operating in a "standards-based" manner, when in fact, very little has changed.

Even if the final policies are not as egregiously off the mark as this one, well-intentioned changes that tinker with the scale instead of the meaning of grades invest a lot of effort in the wrong place. The philosophy behind a policy that a district will no longer give *D*s, for example, usually goes something like this: *D*-level work won't cut it in life, so why should it be acceptable in school? The "no *D*-level work" argument is often based on discussions about compliance in the workplace, where clearly the philosophy has not changed from grading for compliance to grading on achievement. Newspapers quote parent and educator concerns about *D*-level effort and *D*-level work (for example, Hu, 2010) as if they were the same thing, further reinforcing the philosophy of grades as pay earned. Under a no-*D* policy, too, the *A, B, C, F* scale has a wider "failure" range than the *A, B, C, D, F* scale it replaced, for the same underlying achievement continuum.

Sometimes a no-*D* policy is explained as an "*A, B,* or do it over" policy (Hu, 2010), which does sound more like a philosophical change, a realization that grading is supposed to be about learning. In such cases, I recommend that instead of tweaking or repurposing the old grading scale, the district address all of the strategies for grading to support learning listed in figure 3.2 (page 37) and explained in chapters 4 and 5. Addressing the learning-support potential of just the scale without addressing the learning-support potential of other grading strategies will result in incomplete grading reform at best and will leave the door open for the same underlying difficulties (such as grade inflation) to creep back in. As Wiggins (1998, p. 252) observed, "Getting rid of grades lower than *B* makes as little sense as not reporting batting averages under .300."

Learning-Focused Grading Reforms: Communication Is Key

Communication is important for beginning and implementing any new program or procedures, but especially for bringing about changes in grading. Traditional grading habits, practices, and assumptions are deeply rooted in everyone's past history, including those of teachers. Changing to something new affords opportunities to develop shared understandings of grades, because everyone is implementing the same (one hopes!) changes, no matter what their idiosyncratic past experiences and practices looked like.

Arriving at these shared understandings is the first step in pursuing learning-focused grading reforms, and it will require numerous conversations and extensive, ongoing professional development. As I have said repeatedly, these conversations need to be mostly about learning, not about grading. The sea change we are after is not the tweaking of grading mechanisms. The sea change is to think in terms of *learning*—of what students know and can do—instead of *teaching*—what teachers do.

In every district I know that has been successful with grading practice reform, the key conversations have been about learning. Turning-point professional development has been about translating standards into learning targets for students. Ric Williams, director of curriculum and assessment for the Everett Public Schools in Everett, Washington, says: "How do you get your teachers to talk about student learning? Put student work in front of them. In fact, if you do that, try to stop them from talking about student learning" (personal communication, August 24, 2010).

Design and Development of Changes to Grading and Reporting Policies

Communication is important through all stages of the design and development process. Two-way communication between school faculties and district leaders can begin with the aforementioned conversations about grading and learning, move on to commenting on ideas or drafts of documents during design and development, and then continue during the pilot testing phase. Typically, one or a few schools pilot report card and grading policy changes and give feedback to the district's grading committee and other appropriate leaders. After modifications based on the feedback are made, the changes can be implemented districtwide.

Implementation of Changes to Grading and Reporting Policies

During the implementation of new policies, districts often use written documentation in the form of policy statements, guidelines, or teacher handbooks. If the documents are user-friendly, and if they are used, they will contribute to consistency and coordination across classes, grades, and schools. They will also contribute to the development of shared language and procedures, since everyone will be using the same documents. This is in contrast to traditional grading, where grading policies are, as we noted in chapter 5, often limited to a list of cutoff scores for letter grades and directions for computing grade-point averages.

When the Everett Public Schools introduced their new elementary progress reports in 2009 (see fig. 5.3, page 71), they created documents to communicate the new grading policies to educators within the district and explain how to implement them consistently. Everett's "Grading Guidelines" document, shown in figure 6.1, gives teachers guidance in assigning achievement-status grades for the standards listed on the report cards. These guidelines even show teachers how to avoid the temptation to undermine the new grades by "sliding" the scale in various ways (see the ingenious little sections titled "What a '3' is not" and "What a '4' is not"). In doing this, the guidelines use good educational practice themselves. Concepts are clearer when you give both examples and counterexamples than when you just give definitions and examples.

Elementary Progress Report
Everett Public Schools
Grading Guidelines
(8.3.2010)

1. What are the guidelines for giving a '3' or a '4' in the general education classroom?

What a '3' is:

A '3' means the student is <u>meeting</u> the grade-level expectations, i.e., GLEs / PEs. Woohoo! A cause for celebration ☺

What a '3' is not:

A '3' is not for a student who is almost there. Just a little longer and they will have it. This student would be a '2', <u>approaching</u> standard.

What a '4' is:

A '4' means the student's work is <u>exceeding</u> grade-level expectations. In fact, this work is at least one year above grade level.

What a '4' is not:

A '4' is not for a student who did extra "level-3" work for extra credit, or got 100% on tests made up of all level-3 items. Without evidence that the student's work exceeds the grade-level expectations by one year, the student would receive a '3'.

2. What about for students in the Highly Capable Program? What are the guidelines for giving a '3' or a '4' to these high-performing students?

What an 'HC 3' is:

The grade-level expectations (GLEs & PEs) in Reading and Mathematics for students in the Highly Capable Program are one grade level higher. A student <u>meeting</u> these expectations would receive a '3'.

What an 'HC 3' is not:

A '3' is not for a student who is almost there, or is meeting the regular classroom grade-level expectations but not the Highly Capable Program grade-level expectations. This student would be a '2', <u>approaching</u> HC Program grade-level expectations.

What an 'HC 4' is:

A '4' means the student's work is <u>exceeding</u> even the HC Program's grade-level expectations by one year. In Reading and Mathematics, this means the student's performance is exceeding the already-one-grade-level higher expectations by one year.

Figure 6.1: Grading guidelines from the Everett Public Schools.   continued →

What an 'HC 4' is not:	A '4' is not for a student who did extra "HC level-3" work for extra credit, or got 100% on tests made up of all "HC level-3" items. Without evidence that the student's work exceeds the HC Program grade-level expectations by one year, the student would receive a '3'.

3. **How about a student who is a '4' at 1st Trimester but then the performance expectation rises throughout the year to catch up with his/her level. Does that student remain a '4' or drop to a '3'?**

   For example, a student enters Kindergarten knowing all of her letters. Is she a '4'? How about at the end of the year, when the grade-level expectation is for all students to know their letters, is she dropped to a '3'? If so, won't that come across as a drop in performance to her parents?

Skills vs. Standards:	This often appears as a Kindergarten or First Grade issue where a finite number of skills are being measured and reported. Should this student receive a '4' at 1st Trimester? It is the grade-level expectation that students know all of the letters. If a student is meeting that expectation, albeit early, she should get a '3'.
	As one Kindergarten teacher recently told me, "There are 26 letters. It's not like they can know more than 26 letters, or know them better or deeper." We need to be practical in our pursuit of consistency. In this example, if she knows all of the letters (skills), give her a 3 and move on to new expectations where she applies her skills for new learning.

4. **How do we grade a student on an IEP who is performing below grade-level expectations but is performing at his/her achievement level?**

   For example, a third-grade, IEP student is reading at the first-grade level. (1) Does the regular classroom teacher record a '1' on the progress report and let the Resource Room teacher report the student's progress toward his/her IEP Annual Goals, or (2) does the regular classroom teacher modify the grade on the progress report to show how the student is performing on his/her IEP Annual Goals?

   The answer is #1.

Regular Classroom	The regular classroom teacher would report progress on the grade-level expectations (in this example, a '1').
SpEd Resource Room	The SpEd Resource Room teacher would report progress on the student's IEP Annual Goals. This is Special Service's policy and should not be a surprise to parents.

Source: Everett Public Schools, Washington. Used with permission.

Comment Section Guidelines
Elementary Progress Report
Everett Public Schools

Belief Statement:

The comment section of the progress report is the one area where you, as the child's teacher, can provide qualitative and anecdotal information specific to areas of strengths and need unique to the student. It is important to keep in mind these progress reports are read and used by a wider audience than just the student and parent. Progress reports are often included in the body of evidence used to determine program placement in the child's educational future. Your comments also provoke powerful emotions and so therefore provide you an opportunity to invite collaboration, affirm student success, and identify areas of need.

Purpose:

The comment section should be used to provide information about the student as a learner that is not already found in either the progress report itself or in the supplementary material which comprises the full report for parents.

Comments should help further explain:

- Scores which are different than others (e.g. the student is receiving all 3's and 4's but has a 1 in Scientific Inquiry).

- Any score below standard, with a statement from you on strategies employed in the classroom to help address needs.

- Significant changes from scores in a previous reporting period.

- Previous communications you have had with parents--reinforcing, clarifying or reiterating.

- The child's progress in relation to grade-level expectations but also what may be holding him/her back from meeting those standards.

Comments should not:

- Compare the child to his/her peers.

- Convey information that cannot be supported by the evidence you've collected in the classroom.

- State sensitive or confidential information that is better shared in a parent conference.

- Be used to alert the parents to major concerns that have not already been discussed with them previously.

- Describe course content, activities, etc. (refer the parent to the *Learning Across the Year* brochure).

- Convey demands upon parents that do not also include an explanation of how you are addressing needs and challenges in the classroom.

(Please see Comment Exemplars on the back.)

Figure 6.2: Comment guidelines from the Everett Public Schools.   continued →

Comment Exemplars:

Jimmy's additional reading, at school and outside of class, has had a direct and positive impact on his ability to read at standard. In addition to an increase in his vocabulary I am also hearing him use the new science and mathematics vocabulary correctly in classroom discussions and written work.

Maria continues to select only informational texts to read, which is reflected in the lower score in *Reads Different Materials for a Variety of Purposes*. Other reading scores are at or above standard. Please continue to join me in encouraging Maria to widen her reading selections to include fictional material.

Note—the *Complete Classwork on Time* score is a 3 which reflects a terrific improvement from my comment and the score of 1 at the end of the first trimester. Thank you for helping Alaina understand the importance of getting work done during the time provided.

One continued area of growth is Serge's unwillingness to listen to others or to share responsibility for group tasks, especially during math and science table group work. We are practicing daily how to be an effective member of a team.

Since we talked at our October conference, Roberta has been on time to school every day. She is keeping her planner much more organized and up to date with less direct supervision from me—this renewed commitment and independence is making a difference in her learning as evidenced by the recent work she's completed in class.

Jenny's work has improved greatly with the addition of the Alpha Smart for writing usage. She is taking a greater interest in the quality of her work now. We will continue to reinforce creating quality products. Jenny readily accepts feedback from me—remembering to adopt and use the feedback to become a habit is a goal we are working toward.

Willie works hard and is making great strides in mathematics; however, he continues to struggle with adding two digit numbers. To improve his skills in this area I will be providing additional time in class on Math Whizz and basic math skill review. I will also send home materials you can use to help Willie practice his addition.

For a summary of the main topics and skills (Alice) has been studying during this trimester, please refer to the *Learning Across the Year* brochure included with this progress report.

Source: Everett Public Schools, Washington. Used with permission.

An important aspect of these (or any) grading guidelines is the emphasis on student work. The teacher doesn't "give" the 3 or 4; the teacher interprets the student's work as evidence of performance at level 3 or 4. This emphasis on evidence of learning is part of the shift from grading as garnering points to grading to indicate learning.

I suppose you could argue that in a traditional grading context, there was "evidence" too—but it wasn't always evidence of learning. I once heard of a case where a parent complained about her child's report card grade because it was based on only five individual grades—one of which was a pretest and one of which was credit for returning a field trip permission slip to school. To her mind (and mine, too), that meant there were only three legitimate grades. Guidelines such as the ones in figure 6.1 should help avoid problems like this.

The "Comment Section Guidelines" in figure 6.2 arose from observations during Everett's pilot and tryout phase. Analyzing the comments teachers wrote on the new report cards, district leaders found that many of them were about course content, activities, or what the standards entailed, rather than about student learning. The district addressed this in two ways. First, it prepared a brochure for parents, titled *Learning Across the Year*, that included descriptions of what was taught during each trimester. We'll look at that brochure in chapter 7, when we talk about communicating with parents.

Second, the district prepared the "Comment Section Guidelines" to help teachers focus their comments on student learning. The brochure for parents took care of the need for information about course content and activities. Teachers were then free to use the comment section, as the guidelines state, "to provide information about the student as a learner that is not already found in either the progress report itself or in the supplementary material which comprises the full report for parents." To be consistent with the newly emphasized focus on learning (as opposed to teaching) in instruction, assessment, and reporting, the comments in the progress report need to focus on learning as well. The guidelines and comment exemplars are intended to help teachers who are not used to writing learning-focused comments to do just that.

Summary

The main point of this chapter has been that as a district contemplates grading reform, the educators in that district should spend time communicating with one another about what grades should mean. The communication should be ongoing through all stages of the reform process, from contemplating changes, to design, to implementation. The conversations will end up being mostly about learning, rather than grading. Grading reforms get off track when educators talk only about grading methods (things like eliminating *D*s) without tackling the larger question of how their district grades reflect student learning.

Chapter 7

Communicating With Students and Parents

Communication with students and parents about learning should be ongoing. It should definitely not be a once-a-quarter activity. Students and parents should have regular access to information about student achievement, no matter what kind of report card or grading policies are in place. If your school changes report cards or grading policies—for example, from a traditional grading model to a standards-based system—then even more communication is required to help students and parents understand the new system and what its grades mean.

Communicating at the Beginning of the Year

At the start of the school year, it is a good idea to let parents and guardians know what their children will be learning during the year, or at least during the first quarter or report period; how achievement will be graded; and how they can contact you with questions or concerns. It is common for schools or individual classroom teachers to send a letter home at the start of the school year. This is a good time for teachers to communicate their classroom grading policies as well as school and district policies.

Communicating During the Year

During the school year, ongoing communication about student achievement happens in several different ways. Students routinely take work home. Classroom practice work and formative assessments will receive teacher feedback, at least on some of the work, and that will communicate to both students and parents where the student is and where he or she needs to go next. Grades on individual classroom summative assessments—for example, unit tests or papers and projects—communicate information about achievement as well.

Additional communication may take place via telephone, email or school Web portals, and narrative reports or letters. Some teachers use these kinds of communication routinely, for all students. Others, especially middle and secondary teachers responsible for large numbers of students, use these kinds of communication when a special need arises—for example, when a teacher wants to request parent help to work with a student who is having difficulty with a particular kind of work. I recommend that you let your students know at the beginning of the year what your communication patterns will be. We all have heard jokes about teachers calling home to convey good news or congratulations and meeting with the response "What did he do now?"

Communicating at Report Card Time

When you issue report cards, that is the time for additional communication about the meaning of the grades. Even if you sent an initial letter home with students, you should provide the information about grade meaning again at report card time. The principle here is simply timeliness: parents and students will need information about grade meaning at the time they are looking at the grades. They may have kept the first letter, or they may have discarded it, but in any case it's easier and clearer for everyone if information about grade meaning is right at hand when parents and students look at the grades.

Some information about grade meaning should appear directly on the report card. For example, the third-grade report card from the Lincoln Public Schools (see fig. 5.1, page 67) has a gray box at the top of the first page that is a key to the grading symbols used for academic achievement and work/study habits. Another gray box appearing at the bottom of the second page contains the following statements:

> This report offers the best professional judgment about your child's performance in relation to school expectations. It is designed to convey a general view of your child's performance. A more specific report can be gained through a parent-teacher conference. Two conference days are scheduled each year. Additional conferences are welcome.

The district also uses letters and the Internet for home-school communications about grades and grade meaning.

The fourth-grade report card from the Everett Public Schools (see fig. 5.3, page 71) also puts keys for the symbols right on the report card. The "Key for Behaviors That Promote Learning" is printed at the top of the learning behaviors section of the report card. The "Key for Academic Performance" is printed at the top of the academic achievement section of the report card. The key for the progress grades is printed in each row that indicates a progress grade, and the progress grade boxes are shaded to remind readers that the symbols in those boxes are different from the academic achievement grades.

The Everett Public Schools also have a one-page report card supplement that expands on the district's scale definitions. Figure 7.1 shows this document, "Reporting Student Learning Progress." Standards-based grading is a relatively new initiative in the Everett Public Schools, and the district uses this document as a way to explain the initiative and to note that the feedback received from parents and teachers on the pilot version has been used to improve the final report card. The document thanks parents for their feedback; asserts the district's ongoing efforts in aligning curriculum, instruction, and standards; and invites parents to contact their child's teacher with any questions or concerns.

Notice that the Lincoln Public Schools and Everett Public Schools communicate very similar information: the purpose of grades, the meaning of grading symbols, and an open invitation for any questions. There are lots of ways to do this beyond these two examples, but schools must communicate these basic kinds of information. Absent information to the contrary, many parents and students will try to interpret standards-based grades against the system they already know, equating a 4 with an *A* and a 3 with a *B*, for example. Repeated communication and explanation are required for a system to truly change.

As mentioned in chapter 6, the Everett Public Schools also use a parent brochure, titled *Learning Across the Year,* to communicate some of this same basic information. The district has created a different version of the brochure for each elementary grade, K–5, and on the back of each version, it lists more details about the standards for that grade than can be captured on the report card. Figure 7.2 shows the version of the brochure that accompanies the fourth-grade report card shown in figure 5.3 (page 71). This brochure helps parents see what their children are supposed to be learning and also to interpret the academic achievement grades on the report card.

Standards-based report cards may seem very new and different to parents or guardians and community members. I predict that communications that explain grades, grading policies, and standards will be required into the foreseeable future. Even when standards-based grading becomes "old hat" for a given district, it will be different from the grading that is familiar to the previous generation. Without clear communication—and even sometimes despite it—people will interpret grades according to their own previous experiences.

Communicating Beyond the Report Card

There are other ways aside from report cards to communicate about student achievement (current performance status), student progress (improvement, growth, and change), and student behaviors. A complete treatment of these methods is beyond the scope of this book—which is, after all, about grading. However, I believe one important point about these methods is relevant in a book about grading, and thus I will devote a brief section to them here.

Reporting Student Learning Progress

Everett Public Schools

Everett Public Schools has implemented a standards-based elementary progress report which provides more specific information about student performance on the new state and district learning standards. We have reviewed the feedback gathered from teachers and parents and believe the final reporting model described below better communicates student learning and progress to parents. Thank you for your input and support for this new communication tool.

The report summarizes information in three areas:
1. **Behaviors That Promote Learning:** How a student learns.
2. **Academic Performance:** What a student has learned.
3. **Learning Progress:** How much a student has progressed over time.

This is a new way of reporting student progress on state standards and performance expectations. District staff (curriculum specialists, principals and teachers) continue to work hard to align their curriculum and instruction with these new state standards and expectations.

BEHAVIORS THAT PROMOTE LEARNING

This section of the progress report addresses those classroom behaviors which are key to school success, such as cooperation with others, participation in discussions, respect for others, production of quality work, and the effective use of class time.

A student will receive a C, O, S or R to indicate current performance in each area:
C—Consistently
O—Often
S—Sometimes
R—Rarely

ACADEMIC PERFORMANCE

The progress report provides information on a student's current level of performance in Reading, Writing, Communication, Mathematics, Science, Social Studies, Health, Fitness, Music, and Visual Art. The Washington state *Essential Academic Learning Requirements* are provided for each of these content areas, followed by a list of the skills and concepts that represent the end-of-year *Grade Level Expectations*.

A student will receive a 4, 3, 2 or 1 to indicate current performance in each area, based on where a student should be at this point in the school year if on track to meet the Grade Level Expectation by the end of the school year. An asterisk is used when an areas has not yet been taught or evaluated. The brochure, *Learning Across the Year*, shows the learning targets in each academic area for each trimester.

4—**Exceeding** performance expectations by one year at this time
3—**Meeting** performance expectations at this time
2—**Approaching** performance expectations at this time
1—**Below** performance expectations at this time
—(asterisk) Indicates not evaluated at this time*

LEARNING PROGRESS

This section describes a student's progress over time. A student may be performing below expectations for a grade level but still have made significant progress during the last trimester. Alternately, a student may be performing at or above standard academically but only making minimal progress. It is important that students of all developmental ability levels make adequate progress toward meeting or exceeding grade level performance expectations.

A student will receive either a   +   ✓   or   –   to indicate current progress in each area:
+   for **significant** progress
✓   for **steady** progress
–   for **minimal** progress

Parents with questions or concerns are encouraged to contact their student's classroom teacher.

8.3.2010

Source: Everett Public Schools, Washington. Used with permission.

Figure 7.1: Supplementary document for a standards-based report card, describing the meaning of grading symbols.

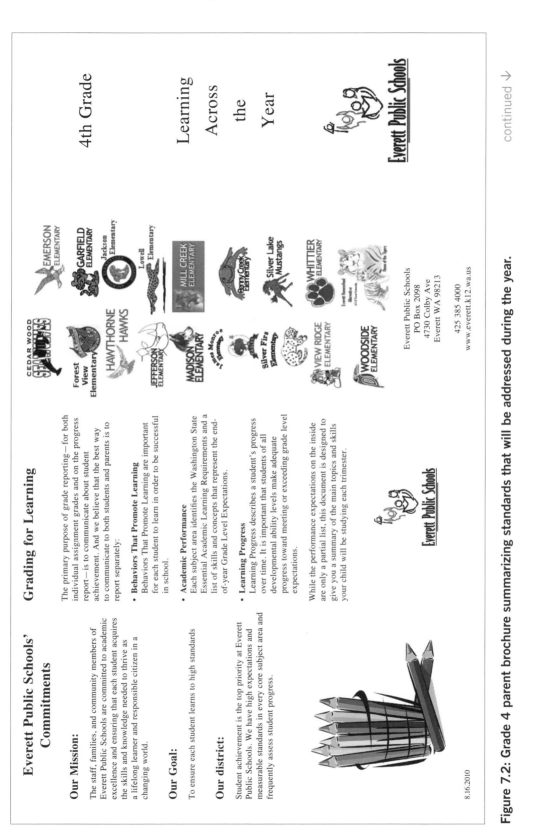

Everett Public Schools' Commitments

Our Mission:

The staff, families, and community members of Everett Public Schools are committed to academic excellence and ensuring that each student acquires the skills and knowledge needed to thrive as a lifelong learner and responsible citizen in a changing world.

Our Goal:

To ensure each student learns to high standards

Our district:

Student achievement is the top priority at Everett Public Schools. We have high expectations and measurable standards in every core subject area and frequently assess student progress.

Grading for Learning

The primary purpose of grade reporting—for both individual assignment grades and on the progress report—is to communicate about student achievement. And we believe that the best way to communicate to both students and parents is to report separately:

• **Behaviors That Promote Learning**
Behaviors That Promote Learning are important for each student to learn in order to be successful in school.

• **Academic Performance**
Each subject area identifies the Washington State Essential Academic Learning Requirements and a list of skills and concepts that represent the end-of-year Grade Level Expectations.

• **Learning Progress**
Learning Progress describes a student's progress over time. It is important that students of all developmental ability levels make adequate progress toward meeting or exceeding grade level expectations.

While the performance expectations on the inside are only a partial list, this document is designed to give you a summary of the main topics and skills your child will be studying each trimester.

4th Grade

Learning Across the Year

Everett Public Schools

EMERSON ELEMENTARY
GARFIELD ELEMENTARY
Jackson Elementary
Lowell Elementary
CEDAR WOOD
MILL CREEK ELEMENTARY
Forest View Elementary
HAWTHORNE HAWKS
Penny Creek Elementary
Silver Lake Mustangs
JEFFERSON ELEMENTARY
MADISON ELEMENTARY
James Monroe
Silver Firs Elementary
WHITTIER ELEMENTARY
VIEW RIDGE ELEMENTARY
WOODSIDE ELEMENTARY

Everett Public Schools
PO Box 2098
4730 Colby Ave
Everett WA 98213

425 385 4000
www.everett.k12.wa.us

8.16.2010

continued ↓

Figure 7.2: Grade 4 parent brochure summarizing standards that will be addressed during the year.

Everett Public Schools   **4th Grade**

First Trimester

Reading
- Selects appropriate books and reads independently for 30 minutes
- Reads fiction and nonfiction texts
- Interprets vocabulary
- Asks questions, predicts, and makes connections while reading
- Distinguishes between important ideas and details
- Reads fluently (smoothness, ease, appropriate pacing)
- Reads DRA book level 40 at an instructional level

Writing
- Generates ideas with details to write stories or provide information
- Organizes ideas logically
- Uses word choice, personal style, and variety of sentence types
- Applies conventions (capitals, punctuation, spelling)
- Writes in narrative or expository form

Mathematics
- Becomes fluent with basic multiplication and related division facts through 10×10
- Represents multiplication of a two-digit number by a one-digit number with place value models
- Identifies factors and multiples of a number
- Multiplies by 10, 100, and 1,000
- Develops efficient procedures for multiplying two- and three-digit numbers
- Interprets simple probabilities and determines/displays results
- Determines the median, mode and range of a set of data and describes what each measure indicates about the data
- Graphs and identifies points in the first quadrant of the coordinate plane

Social Studies
Learns about Civics, Economics, Geography, History and Social Studies Skills while studying:
- Exploring the Pacific Northwest Prior to Statehood
- Living in Washington: Its Geography, Resources, and the Economy
- Being Citizens of Washington

Second Trimester

Reading
- Reads fiction and nonfiction texts
- Interprets vocabulary
- Infers from clues within the reading
- Uses text features (headings, charts, maps, etc.) to gather information
- Analyzes story elements (characters, setting, plot, theme)
- Reads fluently
- Summarizes stories and information
- Reads DRA book level 40 successfully (both fiction and nonfiction)

Writing
- Generates ideas with details to write stories or provide information
- Organizes ideas logically
- Uses word choice, personal style, and variety of sentence types
- Applies conventions (capitals, punctuation, spelling)
- Writes in narrative or expository form

Mathematics
- Represents decimals using place value models, fraction equivalences and number-lines
- Compares and orders decimals and fractions (including mixed numbers) in a variety of ways
- Converts or renames decimals, fractions, and raised numbers
- Simplifies fractions using common factors
- Graphs and identifies points in the first quadrant of the coordinate plane
- Solves single and multi-step problems involving multiplication and/or division and verifies solutions
- Identifies factors and multiples of a number

Social Studies
Learns about Civics, Economics, Geography, History and Social Studies Skills while studying:
- Exploring the Pacific Northwest Prior to Statehood
- Living in Washington: Its Geography, Resources, and the Economy
- Being Citizens of Washington

Third Trimester

Reading
- Reads fiction and nonfiction texts
- Interprets vocabulary
- Visualizes to comprehend while reading text
- Manifests and uses text structures (compare/contrast, cause-effect, etc.) to comprehend the text
- Takes notes for fiction and nonfiction texts
- Thinks critically about the text (the author's role, perspective and style)
- Reads fluently
- Summarizes stories and information
- Reads DRA book level 40 at an independent level (both fiction and nonfiction)

Writing
- Generates ideas with details to write stories or provide information
- Organizes ideas logically
- Uses word choice, personal style, and variety of sentence types
- Applies conventions (capitals, punctuation, spelling)
- Writes in narrative or expository form

Mathematics
- Determines the area and perimeter of a rectangle using formulas
- Solves problems that include perimeter and area
- Performs basic measurement conversions within US customary and metric systems for length, capacity, and weight
- Begins to use algebraic notation
- Fluently multiplies two- and three-digit numbers using the standard multiplication algorithm
- Estimates products to determine reasonableness of answers
- Graphs and identifies points in the first quadrant of the coordinate plane
- Determines elapsed time

Social Studies
Learns about Civics, Economics, Geography, History and Social Studies Skills while studying:
- Exploring the Pacific Northwest Prior to Statehood
- Living in Washington: Its Geography, Resources, and the Economy
- Being Citizens of Washington

Fitness
Learns about Health and Fitness Academic topics including:
Five Components of Fitness activities
- Cardiorespiratory Endurance/Aerobic Activity
- Muscular Strength and Endurance
- Flexibility
- Body Composition/Body Mass Index
- Intensity

Learns about Fitness and develops Motor Skills through:
- Functional or Circuit Training
- Locomotor/Non-Locomotor movements
- Sport Skills
- Organized Activities

Health
- Learns topics of disease control, personal safety, decision making, family/cultural/environmental dynamics, and social skills taught throughout the year

Visual Art
- Plans and creates artwork using the Creative Process
- Communicates ideas and feeling in artwork
- Composes artwork using art elements and principals
- Practices Craftsmanship using art skills and tools

Music
- Reads, writes, and creates notation including pitch names on a staff
- Sings basic harmony in rounds and partner songs
- Plays a pitched instrument
- Gains experience with different kinds and forms of music

Fitness
Learns about Health and Fitness Academic topics including:
- Food for Energy and Health
- Heart Rate
- Goal Setting

Learns about Fitness and develops Motor Skills through:
- Functional or Circuit Training
- Locomotor/Non-Locomotor movements
- Sport Skills
- Organized Activities

Health
- Learns topics of disease control, personal safety, decision making, family/cultural/environmental dynamics, and social skills taught throughout the year

Visual Art
- Plans and creates artwork using the Creative Process
- Communicates ideas and feeling in artwork
- Composes artwork using art elements and principals
- Practices Craftsmanship using art skills and tools

Music
- Reads, writes, and creates notation including pitch names on a staff
- Sings basic harmony in rounds and partner songs
- Plays a pitched instrument
- Gains experience with different kinds and forms of music

Fitness
Learns about Health and Fitness Academic topics including:
- Bone Health
- Muscle Motion

Learns about Fitness and develops Motor Skills through:
- Functional or Circuit Training
- Locomotor/Non-Locomotor movements
- Sport Skills
- Organized Activities

Health
- Learns topics of disease control, personal safety, decision making, family/cultural/environmental dynamics, and social skills taught throughout the year

Visual Art
- Plans and creates artwork using the Creative Process
- Communicates ideas and feeling in artwork
- Composes artwork using art elements and principals
- Practices Craftsmanship using art skills and tools

Music
- Reads, writes, and creates notation including pitch names on a staff
- Sings basic harmony in rounds and partner songs
- Plays a pitched instrument
- Gains experience with different kinds and forms of music

Science—These classes will be offered during the school year:

Reading the Environment
Content
- Provides examples of physical and chemical weathering of rock and describes how the forces of water and wind are major causes of erosion
- Explains how weathering and erosion change the surface of the earth
- Describes an event that could cause the formation of a fossil and infers the conditions that existed at the time the fossil formed

Systems/Inquiry/Application
- Gathers, records, and organizes data
- Shares conclusions from scientific investigations and shows how the conclusions are supported by evidence

Change of State
Content
- Gives examples of water in different states (solid, liquid, and gas) and describes how water can change from one state to another

Systems/Inquiry/Application
- Plans and conducts scientific investigations
- Shares conclusions from scientific investigations and shows how the conclusions are supported by evidence

Land and Water
Content
- Explains the role erosion plays in forming soils, and how erosion can deplete soils
- Describes methods people can use to reduce soil erosion

Systems/Inquiry/Application
- Gathers, records, and organizes data
- Shares conclusions from scientific investigations and shows how the conclusions are supported by evidence

Source: Everett Public Schools, Washington. Used with permission.

Any communication about student achievement, progress, or behavior should be based on evidence. The same evidence process we have described for arriving at report card grades is important for meaningful communication using other methods. I will illustrate this process as it applies to three additional methods of communication: narratives, conferences, and portfolios.

First, however, I will summarize the evidence process itself. We have been referring to this process throughout the book, in our discussion of grades and grading. However, the references to it have been spread over six chapters. Moreover, the evidence process has not been the organizing framework for the treatment of grading, because the theme of this book has been using grading practices that enable you to keep the promise that all your students can learn. So it's a good idea to summarize how that promise, the two key principles of grading on achievement and in ways that support motivation and effort, and the twelve practical strategies all conform to accepted methods of gathering, interpreting, and communicating evidence.

The Evidence Process

Grading, narratives, conferences, and portfolios should be purpose driven, evidence based, and systematic (Brookhart, 2009a). The reason for this is that you want all these communications to be reliable and valid sources of information for parents and students. *Reliable* means you want parents and students to have confidence that the information is accurate and dependable. *Valid* means you want parents and students to find appropriate meaning in these communications, and to be "appropriate," the information has to be appropriate to some purpose.

These are the same qualities that grades should have. Any systematic communication from school to home about a student should have these qualities. The way to ensure these qualities is to go about gathering and communicating evidence in a systematic way. In fact, you should be able to describe the whole process as part of your communication. I have defined the evidence and communication process in the following way (Brookhart, 2009a, p. 176):

1. Set a purpose.

2. Plan the logistics.

3. Collect the evidence.

4. Interpret the evidence.

5. Communicate the information.

6. Listen to the response.

This evidence process is behind report card grades as well as narrative, conference, and portfolio methods of communication. For grading, as well as for these other systematic communication methods, setting the purpose comes first. That's why most of chapter 2 focused on the grading purpose of communicating student achievement of intended learning outcomes or standards. For report card grades, planning the logistics (step 2 of the process) is largely handled at the district level. The format, symbol systems, and timing of report cards, as well as the logistics of sending them home, all reflect district policies.

Chapters 4 and 5 showed how to collect evidence for grading (step 3) and interpret this evidence appropriately (step 4). This information forms the bulk of this book because these processes are the grading strategies teachers and other educators must use if grading is to communicate meaningfully about student learning.

In report card grading, communicating the information (step 5) is a matter of sending home the report card and supplementing it with other information as needed, as discussed earlier in this chapter. I have not said much yet about listening to the responses (step 6). I will talk more about that in the section on conferences. If parents or students have substantive questions or other responses to either individual assignment grades or report card grades, a conference is usually in order.

Narratives

For narrative reporting, you have a wider range of options for purpose than you do with standards-based report cards. Decide before you write what kind of information you want to share: current achievement status or performance; growth, progress, and development; or student classroom processes such as work habits or behavior. Unlike report cards, narratives can also be used for communicating about one subject or a few subjects.

Once you have set your purpose, plan the logistics of how and what you will write. Will it be a letter (sent home with the student or mailed), an email, or something else? Then collect your evidence.

As for grading, make sure you collect relevant evidence. For example, if you want to share current achievement status, you need performance information. If you want to write about a student's work habits, you need systematic observations of the student's working behaviors. The same evidence rules (about getting enough of the right kind of evidence) that apply to grading achievement apply to reporting about students' behaviors. Power and Chandler (1998) suggest that you have two or three weeks of observations if you want to write about student behavior. Their book, *Well-Chosen Words*, is an excellent resource for teachers who want to do narrative reporting.

Interpreting evidence for narrative reports and communicating those interpretations involves writing skill. Instead of assigning a symbol or category (such as 3 or *proficient*), for narratives you are drawing a conclusion or generalization. Usually, these conclusions are in the form of topic sentences in the paragraphs of your narrative, and the rest of each paragraph describes the evidence on which the topic sentence is based. Interpretations of evidence will be more useful if they are more specific. We have all read comments like "Keisha is an excellent student and a pleasure to have in class," which, while enjoyable to read, don't really tell us much.

Responses to narrative comments may come in several forms. Parents may call or email you, or you can follow up narratives yourself with calls or emails to parents. A particularly helpful way to structure responses to narrative communications is for you to suggest ways that the parent or guardian can assist the student at home. Then your follow-up communication can be about supporting that assistance.

Conferences

The nice thing about conferences is that you can engage in conversation with parents, students, or students and parents together—depending on which type of conference you set up. However, a conference is still an official and systematic communication that should start with identifying a purpose. Some conferences are about narrow purposes, for example, a conference with a student about one or a few pieces of writing. Other conferences have fairly broad purposes, for example, a conference with a concerned parent after a report card is issued. Conferences, like narratives, can include discussions of achievement progress, work habits, or other behaviors, as long as you are clear about what your purposes are.

Once you have established purpose(s) for a conference, plan the logistics. Set the date and time, issue invitations, and receive responses about who will be attending. Make sure there are seats for everyone and that the space is comfortable and not intimidating. Hold the conference in a private place and not, for example, at one end of a room where parents of other students are waiting at the other end to talk with you.

Collecting evidence is important for conferences, and I can attest to that myself. As a young middle school teacher, I participated in my school's required parent conferences. I found them very stressful and had a hard time deciding what to say. Somehow it hadn't occurred to me to bring evidence—specific student work about which we could have had great conversations. I brought my gradebook and had the vague purpose "to talk about the grades." It wasn't satisfactory for me or for the parents either, I'm sure. This is one of a very few parts of my early career teaching that I truly wish I could go back and do over again, knowing what I know now about assessment and grading.

With purpose in mind, collect the student work and observational notes that you will use during your conference. If it's a student-led conference, help the student collect the evidence that will be shared. Interpreting evidence for a conference is similar to interpreting evidence for a narrative report. If you lead the conference, your "interpretations" will be conclusions or generalizations about the student's achievement, progress, or work habits and behavior, according to the purpose you set. Then, you support these conclusions by showing and discussing the evidence, the work and/or observations that led you to those conclusions.

If the student is leading the conference, the student will do the interpreting. Typically, student interpretations are standards referenced. For example, a student might say, "I can count to one thousand by fives" or "I can do ten jumping jacks"—and then proceed to demonstrate, right there in the conference. An older student might say, "I can find the area of right triangles, and I can solve real-world and mathematical problems involving the area of right triangles." Then the student would support this claim by showing and describing his or her work, selected and saved for that purpose.

Finally, the great thing about conferences is that the response is not only immediate, but it can be a dialogue. This time, happily, I have a good example from my own career. Not all of those middle school conferences were stressful. In one case, I had a great conference with the father of one of my students that, in hindsight, went well because I did have specific purposes in mind and because both the parent and I were able to listen to each other.

Tosha was twelve years old and in my seventh-grade reading and language arts class. Because her last name was in my section of the alphabet, she was also in my homeroom. Her academic work was good, by any standards, and so were her work habits. She smiled easily and was academically curious. She liked school. When fall conference invitations went out, her father responded that he would be the one who would attend for Tosha.

I wanted to make sure her dad knew two things. First, I wanted him to know that Tosha was definitely college material. Most of the students in my school did not end up going to college. Students who are going to college need to start planning early, so they can, for example, select college-prep courses in high school. I wanted to make sure Tosha made choices that would set her up for college; I wanted to be her early-warning system. Second, on most days Tosha had some issues with body odor. I knew that if that did not change soon, her classmates would begin to tease her. So I wanted to ask her dad to make sure she had clean clothes each day. Talk about setting purpose! I had two purposes, one academic and one behavioral. And I had my evidence: academic evidence for the first purpose and my observations for the second.

It turns out the second purpose was the easy one. Tosha was an only child, and her dad was a single parent. As it happened, doing the laundry was one of Tosha's jobs, and she did it every week. So she knew all about laundry. It was simply time for her to start wearing deodorant, and her dad had been putting off what he thought might be an awkward talk with his daughter. By the very next day, the problem was resolved. Tosha smelled like a flower for the rest of the time I knew her.

More interesting was the surprise on Tosha's father's face when I talked about college. He truly had not thought in those terms. Tosha's family had no experience with college attendance or any of its requirements. So I was able to raise some awareness there, perhaps in a life-changing way. I left that school district at the end of Tosha's seventh-grade year, so I can't tell you whether Tosha went to college or not. I hope she did.

I encourage you to consult additional resources for more information about student-teacher, parent-teacher, or student-parent-teacher conferences. Information about various kinds of conferences can be found in Brookhart (2009a) and in Stiggins (2008). Le Countryman and Schroeder (1996) focus on student-led conferences.

Portfolios

Portfolios can be used for instruction or assessment. If you are interested in using portfolios, I encourage you to read more about them (Arter, Spandel, & Culham, 1995; Hebert, 2001; Nitko & Brookhart, 2011). My goal here is simply to describe how using portfolios for communicating about student learning follows the same six steps that other evidence-based communication methods do.

For portfolios, your purpose decisions will primarily be about the kinds of learning you want to be able to communicate. First, will the portfolio show growth or status? If the portfolio is to show growth in writing, for example, it should include both first and final drafts, as well as writing done over time—hopefully showing improvement. If the portfolio is to show status or accomplishment in writing, it should include a selection of best works, in their final forms. Of course, another purpose decision you make for portfolios is about what domain of learning you want to communicate, for example: writing in general? Narrative writing? Expository, informational writing?

Planning portfolio logistics includes identifying how work is to be collected, where it is to be stored, and how opportunities for student reflection, which is part of the portfolio process (Arter, Spandel, & Culham, 1995), will be structured. You and your students identify what evidence is relevant to the portfolio's purpose and how it will be collected. There are a variety of options here, depending on the amount of structure the teacher builds and how much student choice is allowed.

Interpreting portfolio evidence should always start with the student. Typically, you will ask the student to provide either reflections on each piece of work or reflections on the meaning of the collection of work as a whole. In either case, you can provide a form containing reflection questions to structure the student's interpretation of the meaning of the work in the portfolio.

There are also many options for communicating a message about student achievement using portfolios. You can send portfolios home with instructions for parent-student conversations. You can use them in class as the basis for student-teacher conversations. They can form the basis for parent-teacher or student-parent-teacher conferences. With any of these options, you should plan a mechanism for soliciting and receiving responses. If you send the portfolios home, you can create a response form for questions and follow-up comments. If you use them in conferences, the conversation can be a mechanism for response. Remember to leave time for listening to responses during the conference.

Summary

Communicating with students and parents should happen at the beginning of the school year, throughout the year, and at report card time. Communication methods beyond report cards include narratives, conferences, and portfolios. All of these should be based on an evidentiary process that begins with setting the purpose for the communication. Then, plan the logistics, collect and interpret the evidence, communicate the message and its evidence, and listen to the response. The best communication happens within a conversation, not as a one-way message.

Chapter 8

Assessing Readiness for Grading Reform

I don't know of very many (or any!) school districts in which both the school report cards and every teacher in the system uses standards-based grading, with achievement-only policies featuring a high level of student involvement. This work is just beginning. Important progress has been made, however. In fact, as I look over the history of grading (see Brookhart, 2009a, for more information about the history of grading), it seems to me that we may actually be witnessing a genuinely new development. If we can succeed in establishing achievement-based grading and true student involvement, we will indeed be doing something different with grading than has been reported over the years.

The purpose of this final chapter is to help you contemplate the grading policies and practices you and your school use now. How do you grade individual assignments in your classroom? How do you assign report card grades for your students? What grading practices are you happy with, and which ones are you interested in changing? This chapter will help you reflect on your practices, celebrate what is going well, and move forward with changes.

Your Individual Practices

Where are you now as an individual teacher? Are you operating with a traditional grading model, a performance-based model based on achievement, or something else? What, if any, are your priorities for change? Figure 8.1 will help you reflect on that.

Promising Learning to Your Students

The reflection questions in figure 8.1 start with the philosophical question of how you keep the promise of learning to your students. This is not just because the promise of learning is the theme of this book. In fact, it is the other way around. The promise of learning is the theme because it is the basis from which learning can happen. There has been good evidence for a long time (McLaughlin & Marsh, 1978) that teachers' beliefs that they can make a difference, that they can help even the most difficult or unmotivated students, is the most important factor in school change and in student learning.

Reflect on your current grading practices, including both your own classroom practices and the school and district grading policies with which you must comply. Use figure 3.2 (page 37) as an aid to your reflection in questions 2 and 3.

1. Describe what the implied promise "In my class, in this school, all students can learn" means to you.

2. How closely do your current grading practices uphold the principle that grades should reflect student achievement of intended learning outcomes?

   a. In what ways do your current grading practices support this principle, and in what ways do they not?

   b. What is the most important aspect of the "gap" between grading on achievement and your current practices?

3. How closely do your current grading practices uphold the principle that grading policies should support and motivate student effort and learning?

   a. In what ways do your current grading practices support this principle, and in what ways do they not?

   b. What is the most important aspect of the "gap" between grading on achievement and your current practices?

Figure 8.1: Reflection questions for teachers.

For educators without that belief and promise, no instructional, assessment, or grading practices will be very successful. For educators who do promise learning for their students and believe they can accomplish it, the mission becomes implementing instructional, assessment, and grading practices to support it.

Using Grading to Reflect Learning

Question 2 in figure 8.1 asks how closely your current grading practices uphold the principle that grades should reflect student achievement of intended learning outcomes. How closely do your grading schemes for individual assignments align with Strategies 1 through 6? How closely do your report card grading practices align with Strategies 7 through 12?

Individual Assessments

Your reflections should be about your own grading practices. However, sometimes it's easier to start by considering grading practices other than your own. For example, critique this plan for grading one assignment: An art teacher designed an assignment for her fourth-grade students. They were to make a drawing, on paper, for a quilt patch design. The teacher's learning goals were multidisciplinary. First, she intended her students to demonstrate drawing skills, which she had taught in art class. She also wanted to assess their knowledge of the symbolism used in local quilt patterns, which required an understanding of art as part of culture. This part of the assignment connected with the social studies standards. Here is her grading plan for the quilt patch assignment:

30%: Craftsmanship

30%: Class participation

20%: Following directions

20%: Project design

Arguably, the teacher could grade her students' drawing skills with the craftsmanship criterion, and their use of local quilt symbols with the project design criterion. The teacher gave the students no hint as to how she would allocate points within those 30 percent and 20 percent limits, so we can't evaluate the quality of the information in those portions of the grade. Class participation and following directions are work habits. Therefore, about half (50 percent) of this assignment reflected achievement. The other half reflected nonachievement factors.

The resulting assignment grades would not have reflected achievement very clearly. They couldn't be interpreted as representing what students had learned about art and culture. Enthusiastic participation could cover up for poor understanding of local quilt patterns, for example, or following directions could mask poor drawing skills.

In your reflections on question 2, review the grading schemes for your major tests and performance assessments—projects and other graded assignments that require students to write, construct, or do something. How closely do these grading schemes reflect achievement of intended learning outcomes?

Be honest with yourself. The goal here is for you to understand the grading practices you use, not to "grade" them. In fact, if you feel uncomfortable as you uncover grading practices that might not reflect achievement, and you don't like that feeling, you are still operating from a traditional grading mindset that emphasizes judgment over opportunity to learn. What we're after is an attitude more like "This is what I do, this is what's good about it, this is what I want to change about it, here's how I will do that." That is the same attitude we intend to foster in students by using the learning-oriented, student-centered grading strategies described in this book.

Report Card Grading Practices

Let's continue with the demonstration of how you might reflect on question 2 in figure 8.1. Again, first consider grading practices other than your own.

Critique this high school language arts teacher's plan for combining individual grades for a report card grade: The district report card was in traditional style. There was one row of boxes, one for each quarter (nine weeks), labeled "English/Language Arts." For one of the quarters, the language arts curricular objectives included understanding some grammar and usage principles (conventions of standard English) and reading for meaning (understanding key ideas and details and understanding story structure). Readings were from a literature anthology. Here is the teacher's grading plan for the quarter:

> 30%: Three quizzes, 10% each
>
> 20%: Test
>
> 20%: Paper
>
> 20%: Project
>
> 10%: Homework
>
> Bonus points available

How will achievement be reflected in the resulting grade? In this example, it is really impossible to know. One issue is the components themselves. We don't know what portions of any of the individual grades reflect achievement.

Another issue is the confounding of grades that are really part of the learning process and grades that measure accomplishment or achievement status at the end of instruction. Ten to 40 percent of the list is for "grades" that should reflect practice, not the resulting achievement (homework, 10 percent, and possibly quizzes, 30 percent). I say "possibly quizzes" because whether the quizzes were formative (part of the learning process) or summative (to measure what was learned) depends on how they were used. For example, quizzes given to see whether students had done reading assigned for homework should be used formatively. Quizzes that are truly little tests, announced ahead of time and given after students have worked with the material, can be used for grading.

Yet another issue is the use of bonus points. In a traditional context in which grades are calculated as percentage of points over a base, bonus points mean that different students have different bases for grading. That's not a good way to arrive at meaningful grades. Further, bonus points are often awarded for nonachievement-related work, like helping with classroom supplies. Teachers often use bonus points as a mechanism for not failing a child who was trying (Brookhart, 1993). As such, the bonus points, whatever the teacher tells the student they are for, are for work habits.

Probably the saddest story I ever heard about bonus points is the experience of a friend of mine. He grew up in a big city and attended a poorly resourced junior high school that was labeled "hard to staff." His teachers tried every trick in the book to motivate low-achieving students, including things like giving bonus points if they put their names in the upper right-hand corners of their papers. My friend did that, and he also was a good student. So he often got grades like 104 percent or 106 percent on tests. These grades did not mean advanced achievement. They meant he answered the ordinary, easy test questions correctly and also put his name on his paper. Sad but true. In case you are wondering, the bonus points didn't work to motivate most of his classmates to study. They just muddied the meaning of everyone's grade.

In your reflections on question 2, review your report card grading practices. How closely do your grading plans reflect achievement of intended learning outcomes? Again, be honest with yourself. What elements of your grading practices soundly reflect student achievement? Which ones don't—and why is that? What are the most important gaps between desired and current practice, and what if anything do you want to work on?

Supporting Effort and Motivating Students to Learn

Question 3 in figure 8.1 asks how closely your current grading practices uphold the principle that grades should support and motivate student effort and learning. Here are some questions you might consider in that regard. This isn't an exhaustive list, but it will get you started in the right direction.

- Do your students know at the beginning of the report period how they will be graded in your class? How do you communicate that?

- What opportunities do students have for input into your classroom grading practices?

- Have you ever had a student give up before the end of the report period because there was no way he or she could get a decent (by the student's own definition) grade?

- How do you connect the formative feedback from practice assessments with work on graded assessments?

- How do you handle requests for revisions of work?

- When your students talk about grades, do they also talk about learning?

A fun way to approach this reflection might be for you to think of a story for each question, something like the generalized fictional stories I used at the start of each strategy section in chapters 4 and 5, only about your own students. Much of my thinking about grading has begun by thinking about real stories and wondering what went wrong or how things could be better.

Your School's or District's Practices

As whole schools or districts reflect on their grading practices and explore reform in this area, the philosophy that grades should reflect learning and should help motivate learning (our two principles) should be kept front and center. Whenever I hear of district committees or teachers fussing about whether to forbid zeros, for example, I am sad—because I know they are missing the point. Disagreements about operational bits of a grading plan are often really about philosophical differences. In grading, the main philosophical difference is between those who believe that grades are wages that students earn for compliance with teachers' assignments and requests, and those who believe that grades are indicators of learning and achievement.

To repeat my previous advice—have the fight at that level. Talk about what you really disagree on, and you may be able to resolve it. Compromising about zeros or any other small piece of an overall grading stance will leave the real problem unresolved.

Grading on student achievement is at the heart of any policy designed to support student motivation to learn. If individual graded assignments are supported with opportunities for practice and formative assessment, and if the report card grading policies that combine individual assignment grades into a summary communication are based on known standards of achievement, then students have the information they need to participate in their own learning progress—that is, to be self-determined, self-regulated students who master those known standards. I have also pointed out that this approach is not a magic wand. Students will need coaching to see how this system works, and some students may be so overwhelmed that they will need special help.

What I can promise is that a system of grading based on student achievement has the best chance of supporting self-determination, self-regulation, and a mastery goal orientation in most of the students, most of the time. It certainly has a better chance than a hodgepodge grade (Brookhart, 1991) based on idiosyncratic amounts of achievement, effort, and attitude, depending on the teacher.

Standing firmly in the camp of achievement-based grading, we can add some features to report card grading policies that enhance student involvement. The motivational principle here is self-determination. The more students can be "captains of their own ships" of learning, the more those ships will sail. Let me anticipate at the start a cynical comment that some readers may be forming in their heads, that this sounds more like a mutiny. Stop and think for a moment about the assumptions behind that statement. We should be about empowering students (otherwise, why be in the learning business?), not keeping them captive.

Ways to Begin the Conversation

The reflection questions in figure 8.1 may lead to a sort of "gap analysis": the way grading is done in my school or district does not match the way I would like it to be. This recognition can start with individuals or with teams or groups of colleagues. Sometimes this recognition starts with a perceived need—that curriculum, instruction, and state assessment have gone standards-based and that grading no longer matches. Sometimes there are other agenda items that a district wants to accomplish. For example, the Great Falls Public Schools in Montana are working on changes in grading as part of a long-term systemic change initiative to decrease dropout rates and help more students succeed in school (Tom Moore, personal communication, August 20, 2010). Sometimes a few teachers get interested, as a result of reflection on their own practice, professional development, reading and talking with colleagues, and the like. Often, several of these situations obtain and start the forward motion toward investigating and reforming grading practices.

In any case, there will still be a need for a solid conversation about what grades mean. As one district administrator says, "Everyone tells you to talk purpose first" (see, for example, Guskey & Bailey, 2010). Here are three methods that have been used in various ways by districts with which I am personally familiar and also by districts I have read about. They are not the only methods, but I hope they will give you ideas about how to start grading reform in your context. A variation of one of these ideas might be just the ticket.

Taking Sides and Hearing Them Out

One activity that is suitable for a professional development setting, a school- or departmentwide faculty meeting, or a team meeting is to organize and "fishbowl" a debate. First, select a purpose statement, perhaps the one we are using in this book:

> Grades should reflect student achievement of intended learning outcomes.

Then assign a debate team (four people or so) to take each side, pro and con. In true debate style, participants do not necessarily need to believe in the side they are on but must research and present relevant arguments for their assigned point of view. Give the team members some time to organize their arguments, and then stage the debate while others observe and make notes.

After the debate, open the discussion to the whole group or to small groups at tables if the main group is large. Follow up the conversations with additional readings, discussion, and other professional development.

Form a Committee, and Survey Each School

Districts that have already decided to investigate grading practices and contemplate reform often establish a "grading committee." Purpose discussions should be one of the first items on the committee agenda. Draft a purpose statement and a brief survey about the underlying issues and circulate both documents to the schools with instructions to report back to the committee before its next meeting.

Continue with the process in an iterative manner until every school in the district and every—or almost every—teacher and administrator in the schools can get behind the purpose statement and feels his or her input was heard. Then, start the districtwide conversations about grading policy reform and professional development from there.

Reflect on Readiness for Change

I have met a few people who say that their district's "way in" to talking about purpose and philosophy was to talk about more practical issues. For example, at the district's request, each school could be asked to discuss figure 3.2 (page 37), which displays the practical grading strategies needed to implement the general philosophy of grading on achievement of intended learning outcomes. As I said before, resist the urge to argue about these practical bits. Instead, use the strategies to talk about yourself: Am I ready to do this one? Am I ready to do that one?

Ask individual teachers and administrators to review this list of grading strategies, putting a check next to the ones they agree with and an X next to the ones they disagree with. Advise them to indicate agreement with strategies they like even if they think they need more skill development to be able to apply them. Agreement for this exercise means conceptual buy-in.

Then, compare the checks and Xs from the individual lists. Note the strategies that have unanimous agreement (all checks), and be able to say why. Note those that have unanimous disagreement (all Xs), and be able to say why. Discuss strategies that got mixed responses. What are the issues? What can one learn from them? Then, start the districtwide conversations from there.

Summary

This chapter has discussed assessing readiness for grading reform. In fact, I have tried to encourage it! Assessment of readiness for grading reform can and should occur at two levels: individual and school/district. I have offered methods and tools for engaging in both levels of reflection. I encourage you to use these or devise your own strategies for tackling the big questions about grading purpose, where you and your district are now, and where you want to go.

Keeping the Promise

I started my last book about grading (Brookhart, 2009a, and its previous edition) with the statement "In a perfect world there would be no grades" (p. 2). I still believe that. In a utopia, learning is a pure good. Students learn because it's the right thing to do, both for themselves and for the society in which they live; students learn because it's fun and interesting; students learn to the best of their abilities and capacities; and everyone learns something useful, whether it's the same thing as their classmates or not. In a utopia, grades are irrelevant.

Since we don't expect that utopia to exist any time soon, the best we can do is give grades that serve learning and then use them to feed back into the learning. We use grades to communicate so parents and students can help that happen. We use grades to help students (and ourselves) plan ever more useful and appropriate learning opportunities in our present and future classes. Grading is a means to an end. I wanted to make sure to say that loud and clear. In a book focused on grading, it would be easy to leave the impression that grading is a goal in itself, and I don't want to do that. Grading should be instrumental to learning.

Similarly, because I have advocated so strongly for grading that reflects learning, it would be easy to leave the impression that these standards-based grading methods are the best thing since sliced bread and, if implemented properly, will address all current concerns about learning and about accounting and communicating that learning. I don't want to do that either.

Grading methods that support learning will address *many* current concerns. The first section of this book showed that when grades are *information about learning*, they become powerful supports for learning and supports for effort and motivation. A theme of this book has been to grade in such a way that students have some measure of control over their grades and their learning, and that will help learning and motivation, too.

These methods are the best we have, but they are not silver bullets. Marzano (2010) points out that in a truly standards-based world, students who were not proficient would not move on until they met the standard. So "standards-based grading" might more properly be called "standards-referenced grading," because performance is reported with reference to standards. True standards-based grading is reminiscent of mastery grading (Morrison, 1926/1992) and mastery learning (Bloom, Hastings, & Madaus, 1971).

Mastery learning didn't work on a large scale then, and it probably wouldn't work on a large scale now. In addition to the planning, teaching, and reporting issues that arise when each student is working at something different, Wiggins (1998) reminds us that two typical results of trying to execute mastery learning in many curricular domains were grade inflation and oversimplification of standards—boiling them down to performance on small-grain-sized assessments.

Mastery learning is, in fact, great for learning goals that, in their best form, do represent small-grain-sized accomplishments. For example, a piano student learning to play two octaves of the C-major scale (no sharps or flats), with both hands, keeps practicing that scale until she can do just that. Only then does she move on to the F-major scale (one flat), the next most difficult one. But most current standards for school learning (for example, the Common Core State Standards) do not describe this small-grain-sized learning. Rather, they describe more complex kinds of things, like learning some concepts in a certain content domain and being able to use them to reason, write, or solve problems. If educators try to boil complex learning goals down into small-sized ("master-able") packages, they compromise the learning goals.

Therefore, it is almost inevitable that you will sometimes assign "standards-based" grades that indicate a student did not, in fact, reach proficiency or learn what you intended for him to learn, and yet you will move on. Neither adopting standards-based grading nor adapting traditional grading practices to better represent student learning will *guarantee* that all students learn. Grading is just one more tool.

The theme of this book is that adopting standards-based grading or, short of that, at least adapting traditional grading practices to better represent student learning will give the best information about learning to you and to students and parents. This is your best shot at keeping the promise that in your classroom, in your school, all students can learn. It is your best shot at maximizing student learning and supporting the effort and motivation needed for students to regulate their own learning. That in itself is a lot—and well worth your time and energy. But it will not, single-handedly, save the world.

I hope these two final disclaimers do not dampen your interest in improving grading practices. I hope, rather, that they put the book in perspective and make the grading practices outlined here seem even more sensible, framing them as the best we have to offer our students. I hope that some readers now feel motivated to start experimenting with learning-oriented, student-centered grading practices in their own contexts.

To encourage you to take this leap, I will close with a story of a real-life district whose efforts can serve as a model and an inspiration.

The Journey to Learning-Focused Grading

In the process of writing this book, I was excited to find out about the work of the Spokane Public Schools that began in 2006. I interviewed Tammy Campbell, executive director of Teaching and Learning Services for the Spokane Public Schools, and Mary Weber, former principal of Adams Elementary School and current principal of Grant Elementary School in Spokane. Both of them said I could tell their stories if I also emphasized to my readers that they didn't act alone. Changing grading practices in Spokane was a real team effort and reflects the work of the entire staff.

The story of the Spokane Public Schools shows how grading reform works when the focus remains squarely on learning. Since 2006, this district has been on a journey from traditional to standards-based elementary school report cards and learning-focused grading practices. It is planning to tackle secondary grading next. The district's story is an independent example that supports the grading principles and strategies I have been writing about. Spokane's grading reform work predates this book. The work is theirs. I had nothing to do with it. I hope it will inspire you.

Of course there is more to the story than I can report here. I have selected some highlights from the district's journey that illustrate some of the themes in this book. The information comes from interviews with Tammy Campbell (July 12, 2010) and Mary Weber (July 22, 2010). Any errors of omission or commission are my own.

How It Started

Tammy Campbell, co-chair of the grading committee, reports that the Spokane Public Schools had already moved to a standards-based instructional model when the whole issue of grading arose. And of course the Washington state test was based on state standards. Teachers observed the disconnect here. In this standards-based, "written-taught-tested" model, how did status quo report cards fit? The answer: they didn't. After two years of hearing comments about this from around the district, in 2006 the district put together a committee that included one representative from every school. About half were administrators, and half were classroom teachers. Parents were on the committee, too. In addition, the district partnered with the Spokane Education Association, because grading changes involved teacher workload issues.

When Tammy and her colleagues tried to set up a grading committee, they encountered some understandable "baggage" from previous district committee work. Mary Weber, a veteran teacher and administrator, reports that her first reaction was, "I'm not going to be on that committee. I was around ten years ago [on a previous grading committee], when they couldn't decide what an *A* or a *B* was." The last thing Mary wanted to do, she said, was to change a report card, which she described as "grabbing the lion by the tail."

Professional Development

During the first year, Tammy and others went to workshops and visited districts that had already experimented with changing their report cards and grading policies and practices. Around the district, they used professional development materials by Stiggins, Danielson, and Marzano. Interestingly, most of the professional development centered on learning targets, formative assessment, and student work—not grading per se. This emphasis on student work resonates with the experience of the Everett Public Schools reported earlier.

At Adams Elementary School, Mary Weber and her staff also did professional development on assessment for learning and worked to develop a community of professional learners. Mary reports that she was even able to see a veteran staff member, previously very resistant to change, look at assessment for learning in a new way. In fact, Adams staff members got excited about the prospect of changing assessment in general, and a counselor asked if they could submit an application for a grant being offered for schools to do student-led conferencing.

As year two started, the committee worked on a purpose statement for grading, using the "loop-in, loop-out" method. The committee worked on a draft purpose statement, sent it to schools for feedback, and made changes based on that feedback. The committee also circulated a list of Six Principles of Grading, based on the work of Marzano and Danielson; got feedback; and made changes. As Tammy says, "The teachers wordsmithed them and came up with examples that lived in our system."

I love that phrase "examples that live in our system." It gives a much broader context to the idea of ownership. So often you hear people talk about "ownership" in a more egotistical way, assuming that people won't buy into an idea unless they feel they personally invented it. Really, ownership in this sense should mean the feeling that the idea is *right for us*, that it fits the context in which we teach and our students learn. The iterative process not only helped create shared ownership but was also a way that the committee members deliberately worked to make sure they "did not get too far ahead of the rest of the district."

Also during year two, Tammy began to work with a programmer to design an electronic record book that would enable people to do standards-based grading. In retrospect, she says that if she had it to do over again, she would begin working with the programmer sooner in the process.

Communication was a big emphasis in Spokane's grading reform efforts. Committee members had assignments to go back to their schools and share with staff what the committee had done. Principals did this, too. Also as part of the communication process, the district sent out an annual parent survey about grading, starting in year one. At the end of each year, every school made a brief video to share its work. By the end of year two, the committee had draft report cards ready. These, too, were looped out to schools for discussion and feedback.

Seven schools were selected to pilot the draft report cards, based on their self-assessed readiness for standards-based grading. The district used a readiness rubric and set a criterion of at least 90 percent staff buy-in for the school to be part of the pilot. During the pilot year, teacher record keeping required intensive handwork because the electronic record book was not ready yet. That turned out to be very time-consuming for staff, but also very useful. Tammy characterized the first trimester as "brutal" because of the work involved.

Teachers designed and redesigned forms and other record-keeping tools, including forms to record student performance on assessments clustered by standard. These teacher-designed tools informed the programmer's design work. The end result was a more useful electronic record book and a handbook for teachers that included the tools. Other components of the teacher handbook were lists of standards by grade and trimester and cut scores on common assessments when applicable.

In 2009–2010, after a year of pilot testing, the elementary report cards "went live"—they were put into use in all the elementary schools in the district. The electronic record book was operational by that time, having come online by the end of the pilot year. In May at the end of year three, the district required every school that was not a pilot school to participate in training to learn about the new system. Pilot teachers led the training, which was conducted by grade level and used the handbook. In addition, there were workshops in November of 2009, and after that, as Tammy says, "It was okay." One of the elements of the new system was learning-focused grading practices, as have been outlined in this book. Another element was the use of common assessments to count for about 30 percent of students' grades. The purpose was consistency in measurement.

Communication within the district continued to be a priority. Tammy credits the success of the project to the fact that she and the committee kept going back to teachers, asking what they needed, and working to meet those needs. During development and piloting, any reasonable request, she said, was considered and accommodated. This represented a lot of effort on the part of both the grading committee and central administration. Then, during the May rollout to the whole district, Tammy attended each grade's training workshop and took notes on any grumblings. She reports, "I messaged over and over, 'You may be right, but we can't let our pursuit of perfection paralyze us. On our worst day in standards-based [grading], we're better than on our best day in the other system, because our grades then weren't meaningful.'" The result of this inventory of grumblings was the addition of an FAQ section to the teachers' handbook.

Communication with parents also continued. In March of year four, 98 percent of parents in the district reported that the grades on their children's report cards matched what they heard at parent conferences and saw in students' portfolios.

Meanwhile, back at Adams Elementary School, the staff members had accomplished their pilot test year with an extra twist. They did get that grant to introduce student-led parent conferences, and so Adams plunged into two innovations at once: standards-based grading and student-led conferences. Over the course of a week of open house meetings, the principal, Mary Weber, spoke with 185 of the 240 families in the school. She described what they were doing with both grading and conferencing and why they were doing it.

Even kindergartners did student-led conferences. The learning targets were posted, students demonstrated for their parents what the target was, and teachers could show parents how to interact with their children on that target. For example, teachers could describe to parents how to read with their children or how to count with them. The community became more educated about what was going on in school, and achievement increased dramatically.

In my interview with Mary, she was candid about some delicate issues. She pointed out that the only people who don't like standards-based grading are parents of "kids who can get straight *A*s by just showing up." Adams Elementary had been used to giving out all sorts of awards: first honor roll, second honor roll, and so on. Awards took up a lot of their time. Parents came to assemblies, but it was always the same group of students who won the awards. As part of the move to standards-based grading, Adams suspended these grade-based awards and turned the focus instead to learning, not ranking. This was scary territory for Mary and her staff. She said, "When this [using standards-based report cards] all started, I really spent the summer not sleeping. I had to not be afraid to deal with this. We had teachers still grading on whether students' homework was in, and we had homeless students. Now, every student can make growth and show they've made growth with their portfolios."

The standards-based practices that the parents of "*A* for showing up" students feared would jeopardize their little darlings' star status actually wound up helping those students. A focus on reporting learning revealed that their learning needs weren't being met. Teachers could no longer just give these students an *A* and call it good. They had to deal with ways to teach and get evidence about advanced-level performance.

I asked Mary whether advanced work usually meant letting students go deeper with the grade-level standards or move on to another standard. She replied, "My strongest teachers have students go deeper on the same standard. Some go on." She says she encourages her teachers to "use that 4 category: consistently outperforms the standards." In order for teachers to have evidence of that level of performance, students need to do challenging work, not just get 100 percent on regular work.

Unresolved Issues

In fact, this is one issue that both Tammy and Mary said was still unresolved, and it's an issue I encourage you to grapple with. In a standards-based, learning-focused context, what is the difference between a 4 and a 3, or between advanced and proficient? *Advanced* should not mean just doing 100 percent of the tasks or answering 100 percent of the questions that demonstrate proficiency. *Advanced* should mean engaging with the standards at a level beyond proficiency for that grade level. Most ordinary assessments are not really designed to help students show advanced performance.

I should also point out that the same principle operates at the 1 and 2 levels of performance—the basic and partially proficient levels (or whatever term your district uses for those levels). A partially proficient student should not be labeled as such because he or she did a half-baked job on tasks that demonstrate proficiency or incorrectly answered a portion of test questions written at the proficient level. To be well measured, a student at the partially proficient level of performance should also *correctly* answer test questions written at that less-than-proficient level or do tasks that satisfactorily indicate that level of performance (Norman & Buckendahl, 2008). Again, most ordinary assessments are not really designed to do this.

This brings us back to our theme that it's about learning. Only some of the work of reforming grading is about grading itself. Much of the work that needs to be done is about learning: what will students learn, and how will they show you they have learned it?

Where Will You Go Next?

What is ahead for you? Perhaps you want to work on some of the ideas in this book with colleagues in your school or district. As Dr. Seuss predicted, "Oh, the places you'll go!" As you work to make your grades reflect student achievement of intended learning outcomes and work toward grading policies that support and motivate student effort and learning, you will also help enact that implicit promise you made when you stepped into a classroom: *in my class, in this school, all students can learn.*

References

Ames, C., & Archer, J. (1988). Achievement goals in the classroom: Students' learning strategies and motivation processes. *Journal of Educational Psychology, 80*, 260–267.

Arter, J., Spandel, V., & Culham, R. (1995). *Portfolios for assessment and instruction.* ERIC Digest EDO-CG-95-10. (ERIC Document Reproduction Service No. ED388890)

Au, W. (2007). High stakes testing and curricular control: A qualitative metasynthesis. *Educational Researcher, 36*(5), 258–267.

Bandura, A. (1997). *Self-efficacy: The exercise of control.* New York: W. H. Freeman.

Bloom, B., Hastings, J. T., & Madaus, G. F. (1971). *Handbook on formative and summative evaluation of student learning.* New York: McGraw-Hill.

Boekaerts, M. (1999). Self-regulated learning: Where we are today. *International Journal of Educational Research, 31*, 445–457.

Brennan, R. T., Kim, J., Wenz-Gross, M., & Siperstein, G. N. (2001). The relative equitability of high-stakes testing versus teacher-assigned grades: An analysis of the Massachusetts Comprehensive Assessment System. *Harvard Educational Review, 71*, 173–216.

Brookhart, S. M. (1991). Letter: Grading practices and validity. *Educational Measurement: Issues and Practice, 10*(1), 35–36.

Brookhart, S. M. (1993). Teachers' grading practices: Meaning and values. *Journal of Educational Measurement, 30*, 123–142.

Brookhart, S. M. (1994). Teachers' grading: Practice and theory. *Applied Measurement in Education, 7*, 279–301.

Brookhart, S. M. (1999a). Teaching about communicating assessment results and grading. *Educational Measurement: Issues and Practice, 18*(1), 5–13.

Brookhart, S. M. (1999b). The art and science of classroom assessment: The missing part of pedagogy. *ASHE-ERIC Higher Education Report, 27*(1). Washington, DC: The George Washington University Graduate School of Education and Human Development.

Brookhart, S. M. (2004). *Grading.* Upper Saddle River, NJ: Pearson Education.

Brookhart, S. M. (2008). *How to give effective feedback to your students.* Alexandria, VA: Association for Supervision and Curriculum Development.

Brookhart, S. M. (2009a). *Grading* (2nd ed.). Upper Saddle River, NJ: Pearson Education.

Brookhart, S. M. (2009b). The many meanings of "multiple measures." *Educational Leadership, 67*(3), 6–12.

Brookhart, S. M., Andolina, M., Zuza, M., & Furman, R. (2004). Minute math: An action research study of student self-assessment. *Educational Studies in Mathematics, 57*, 213–227.

Bursuck, W. D., Munk, D. D., & Olson, M. M. (1999). The fairness of report card grading adaptations. *Remedial and Special Education, 20*, 84–92, 105.

Bursuck, W. D., Polloway, E. A., Plante, L., Epstein, M. H., Jayanthi, M., & McConeghy, J. (1996). Report card grading and adaptations: A national survey of classroom practices. *Exceptional Children, 62,* 301–318.

Butler, D. L., & Winne, P. H. (1995). Feedback and self-regulated learning: A theoretical synthesis. *Review of Educational Research, 65,* 245–281.

Common Core State Standards Initiative. (2010a). *Common core state standards for English language arts & literacy in history/social studies, science, and technical subjects.* Accessed at www.corestandards.org/assets/CCSSI_ELA%20Standards.pdf on March 29, 2011.

Common Core State Standards Initiative. (2010b). *Common core state standards for mathematics.* Accessed at www.corestandards.org/assets/CCSSI_Math%20Standards.pdf on March 29, 2011.

Conley, D. T. (2000, April). *Who is proficient? The relationship between proficiency scores and grades.* Paper presented at the annual meeting of the American Educational Research Association, New Orleans. ERIC Document No. ED 445025

Cox, K. B., & Olsen, C. (2009, April). *Putting classroom grading on the table: A reform in progress.* Paper presented at the annual meeting of the American Educational Research Association, San Diego.

D'Agostino, J., & Welsh, M. (2007). *Standards-based progress reports and standards-based assessment score convergence.* Paper presented at the annual meeting of the American Educational Research Association, Chicago.

Dweck, C. S. (2000). *Self-theories: Their role in motivation, personality, and development.* New York: Psychology Press.

Evans, E. D., & Engelberg, R. A. (1988). Student perceptions of school grading. *Journal of Research and Development in Education, 21*(2), 45–54.

Frisbie, D. A., & Waltman, K. K. (1992). Developing a personal grading plan. *Educational Measurement: Issues and Practice, 11*(3), 35–42.

Gronlund, N. E., & Brookhart, S. M. (2009). *Gronlund's writing instructional objectives* (8th ed.). Upper Saddle River, NJ: Pearson Education.

Guskey, T. R., & Bailey, J. M. (2001). *Developing grading and reporting systems for student learning.* Thousand Oaks, CA: Corwin Press.

Guskey, T. R., & Bailey, J. M. (2010). *Developing standards-based report cards.* Thousand Oaks, CA: Corwin Press.

Guskey, T. R., Swan, G., & Jung, L. A. (2010, May). *Developing a statewide, standards-based student report card: A review of the Kentucky initiative.* Paper presented at the Annual Meeting of the American Educational Research Association, St. Louis, MO.

Hebert, E. A. (2001). *The power of portfolios: What children can teach us about learning and assessment.* San Francisco: Jossey-Bass.

Hu, W. (2010, August 7). Little as they try, students can't get a D here. *New York Times.* Accessed at www.nytimes.com/2010/08/08/education/08grades.html on March 9, 2011.

Huntsinger, C. S., & Jose, P. E. (2009). Parental involvement in children's schooling: Different meanings in different cultures. *Early Childhood Education Quarterly, 24,* 398–410.

Jung, L. A. (2009). The challenges of grading and reporting in special education. In T. R. Guskey (Ed.), *Practical solutions for serious problems in standards-based grading* (pp. 27–40). Thousand Oaks, CA: Corwin Press.

Jung, L. A., & Guskey, T. R. (2007). Standards-based grading and reporting: A model for special education. *Teaching Exceptional Children, 40*(2), 48–53.

Jung, L. A., & Guskey, T. R. (2010). Grading exceptional learners. *Educational Leadership, 67*(5), 31–35.

Kagan, S. (1989/90). The structural approach to cooperative learning. *Educational Leadership, 47*(4), 12–15.

Kagan, S. (1995). Group grades miss the mark. *Educational Leadership, 52*(8), 68–71.

Le Countryman, L., & Schroeder, M. (1996). When students lead parent-teacher conferences. *Educational Leadership, 53*(7), 64–68.

Marzano, R. J. (2010). *Formative assessment and standards-based grading.* Bloomington, IN: Marzano Research Laboratory.

McElligott, J., & Brookhart, S. (2009). Legal issues of grading in the era of high stakes accountability. In T. R. Guskey (Ed.), *Practical solutions for serious problems in standards-based grading* (pp. 57–74). Thousand Oaks, CA: Corwin Press.

McLaughlin, M. W., & Marsh, D. D. (1978). Staff development and school change. *Teachers College Record, 80,* 69–94.

Morrison, H. C. (1992). The practice of teaching in the secondary school. In Laska, J. A., & Juarez, T. (Eds.), *Grading and marking in American schools: Two centuries of debate* (pp. 45–52). Springfield, IL: Charles C Thomas. (Original work published 1926)

Moss, C. M., & Brookhart, S. M. (in press). *Learning targets: The key to formative assessment and differentiated instruction.* Alexandria, VA: Association for Supervision and Curriculum Development.

Nitko, A. J., & Brookhart, S. M. (2011). *Educational assessment of students* (6th ed.). Boston: Pearson Education.

Norman, R. L., & Buckendahl, C. W. (2008). Determining sufficient measurement opportunities when using multiple cut scores. *Educational Measurement: Issues and Practice, 27*(1), 37–46.

Nuthall, G. (2005). The cultural myths and realities of classroom teaching and learning: A personal journey. *Teachers College Record, 107*(5), 895–934.

O'Connor, K. (2009). *How to grade for learning K–12* (3rd ed.). Thousand Oaks, CA: Corwin Press.

O'Connor, K. (2011). *A repair kit for grading* (2nd ed.). Boston: Pearson Education.

Pajares, F. (1996). Self-efficacy beliefs in academic settings. *Review of Educational Research, 66*(4), 543–578.

Perie, M. (2008). A guide to understanding and developing performance-level descriptors. *Educational Measurement: Issues and Practice, 27*(4), 15–29.

Perry, N., Phillips, L., & Dowler, J. (2004). Examining features of tasks and their potential to promote self-regulated learning. *Teachers College Record, 106,* 1854–1878.

Power, B. M., & Chandler, K. (1998). *Well-chosen words: Narrative assessments and report card comments.* York, ME: Stenhouse.

Reeves, D. B. (2004). The case against the zero. *Phi Delta Kappan, 86*(4), 324–325.

Ryan, R. M., & Deci, E. L. (2000). Self-determination theory and the facilitation of intrinsic motivation, social development, and well-being. *American Psychologist, 55*(1), 68–78.

Sanders, W. (1998). Value-added assessment. *School Administrator, 55*(11), 24–27.

Scriffiny, P. L. (2008). Seven reasons for standards-based grading. *Educational Leadership, 66*(2), 70–76.

Seidel, T., Rimmele, R., & Prenzel, M. (2005). Clarity and coherence of lesson goals as a scaffold for student learning. *Learning and Instruction, 15,* 539–556.

S.G.B. (1992). Weekly reports in schools. In J. A. Laska & T. Juarez. (Eds.), *Grading and marking in American schools: Two centuries of debate* (pp. 11–14). Springfield, IL: Charles C. Thomas. (Original work published in 1840)

Stiggins, R. (2008). *Student-involved assessment FOR learning* (5th ed.). Upper Saddle River, NJ: Pearson Education.

Stiggins, R. (2009). Foreword. In K. O'Connor (Ed.), *How to grade for learning K–12* (3rd ed., pp. ix–x). Thousand Oaks, CA: Corwin Press.

Talley, N. R., & Mohr, J. I. (1993). The case for a national standard of grade weighting. *Journal of College Admissions, 139,* 9–13.

Taylor, C. S., & Nolen, S. B. (2005). *Classroom assessment.* Upper Saddle River, NJ: Pearson Education.

Waltman, K. K., & Frisbie, D. A. (1994). Parents' understanding of their children's report card grades. *Applied Measurement in Education, 7,* 223–240.

Welsh, M. E., & D'Agostino, J. V. (2009). Fostering consistency between standards-based grades and large-scale assessment results. In T. R. Guskey (Ed.), *Practical solutions for serious problems in standards-based grading* (pp. 75–104). Thousand Oaks, CA: Corwin Press.

Wiggins, G. (1998). *Educative assessment: Designing assessments to inform and improve student performance.* San Francisco: Jossey-Bass.

Wiggins, G., & McTighe, J. (2006). *Understanding by design* (Expanded 2nd ed.). Upper Saddle River, NJ: Pearson Education.

Willingham, W. W., Pollack, J. M., & Lewis, C. (2002). Grades and test scores: Accounting for observed differences. *Journal of Educational Measurement, 39,* 1–37.

Winger, T. (2005). Grading to communicate. *Educational Leadership, 63*(3), 12–15.

Winger, T. (2009). Grading what matters. *Educational Leadership, 67*(3), 73–75.

Index

A

accommodations, 35
Adams Elementary School, Washington, 30, 137
analytic rubrics, 51
assessments
    blueprint, 49–50, 75
    formative, 7, 31–33, 54–56
    high quality, ensuring, 44–54
    relationship between grading, reporting information and, 7–8
    student, 7–8
    summative, 7
    use of term, 7
attendance, 78

B

behavioral issues, handling, 58–60
blueprint assessment, 49–50, 75

C

Campbell, T., 137–141
Chandler, K., 121
classroom versus district grading policies, 79–81
College Board, 19–20
College Board Standards for College Success, 19
Common Core State Standards, 19
communication
    clear learning targets, 41–44
    grading reforms and importance of, 105–111
    process, 120–121
communication with students and parents
    beginning of school year, 113
    conferences, 122–124
    narratives, 121–122
    ongoing, during the school year, 113–114
    portfolios, 124–125
    reliability and validity of, 120
    at report card time, 114–115
communities, grading views of, 9
completion/fill-in items, writing, 46
conferences, 122–124
Content Knowledge, 19
content standards, 18–20
Council of Chief State School Officers, 19
curriculum standards, 20–22

D

D'Agostino, J., 16
Danielson, C., 138
differentiated instruction, 34
district policies, classroom versus, 79–81
districts, readiness for grading reform, 132–134

E

essay items, writing, 47–48
evaluations
    peer, 61–62
    use of term, 6–7
Everett Public Schools, Washington, 66, 71–73, 106–110, 114–115, 116–119

evidence
    blending of, 88–98
    borderline cases, 97–98
    conferences, 122–124
    evaluating, for final grades, 90–98
    failure to try, distinguishing, 94–97
    forms for, 83–84
    how much should be recorded, 83
    mean versus averages, 90
    median, 91–93
    methods for, 84–86
    multiple measures, 86–88
    narratives, 121–122
    portfolios, 124–125
    process, 120–121
    recency of, 89, 93–94
    weighting, 89
    what should be recorded, 82–83
external motivation, 25

F

feedback, use of, 61
formative assessments
    defined, 7
    motivation and self-regulations and, 31–33
    using, before grading, 54–56

G

grades
    how not to use, 4–5
    making meaningful, 56
    purpose of, 3–4
    reporting, 82–86
    use of term, 6
grading on standards for achievement
    benefits for teaching and learning, 17–18
    importance of, 15–18
    research on, 15–17

grading policies
    classroom versus district, 79–81
    clearly stating, 78–82
    external pressures on, 9–10
    higher education pressure, 10
    normative, 9
    parents and community views of, 9
    reasons for documenting, 81–82
    relationship between reporting information, assessment and, 7–8
    self-reflection, 10–12, 14
grading reforms
    importance of communication and, 105–111
    readiness for, 127–134
    schools or districts, readiness for, 132–134
    teachers, readiness for, 127–131
grading scale policies, changes in, 103–105
group grades, avoiding, 62–63
Guskey, T. R., 36

H

higher education pressure on grading policies, 10
holistic rubrics, 51, 52
homework, preparing students for, 58

I

I Can statements, 30
individual assignment grades
    group work and, 63
    self-reflection, 14
    strategies for, 37, 60–62
    use of term, 6
internal motivation, 25–26
involving students with grading, 98–99

J

Jung, L. A., 35–36

K

Kagan, S., 62

L

learning, building a grading system that supports, 22–24
learning outcomes, 20–22
  identifying, 42–43
  matching instruction to, 50
learning targets
  communicating clear, 41–44
  defined, 30
Le Countryman, L., 124
Lincoln Public Schools, Nebraska, 66, 67–68–70, 114, 115

M

marks. *See* grades
Marzano, R., 135, 138
mastery learning, 135–136
matching items, writing, 46
Mid-continent Research for Education and Learning (McREL), 19
Minute Math, 29
modifications, 35
motivation
  differentiated instruction, 34
  external, example of, 25
  formative assessment, 31–33
  grading strategies, 36–38
  I Can statements, 30
  internal, 25–26
  Minute Math, 29
  reflective journals/tools, 30–31
  self-determination, 25–26
  self-efficacy, 26
  self-regulation, 26, 28–33
  supporting students', 27–28
multiple-choice items, writing, 46–47

multiple measures, 86–88

N

narratives, 121–122
National Academy of Sciences, 20
National Council for the Social Studies, 20
National Council of Teachers of English, 20
National Council of Teachers of Mathematics, 20
National Governors Association Center for Best Practices, 19
National Science Teachers Association, 20
nonachievement factors
  attendance, 78
  handling, 59–60
  reporting, 75–76
  scales for, 76–78
no-zero policy, 104

O

O'Connor, K., 6

P

parents, grading views of, 9
Partnership for 21st Century Skills, 61
peer evaluations, 61–62
performance standards, 18–20
portfolios, 124–125
Power, B. M., 121
process criteria, 35
product criteria, 35
progress criteria, 35

R

record-keeping. *See* reporting grades
Reeves, D. B., 94
reflective journals/tools, 30–31
reliability
  communication, 120

defined, 6

report card grades

    self-reflection, 14

    standards-based, 23–24, 65–73

    strategies for, 37–38

    traditional, and standards-based, 23–24

    use of term, 6

report cards, format of, 65

reporting grades

    blending of evidence for, 88–98

    forms for, 83–84

    how much should be recorded, 83

    methods for, 84–86

    what should be recorded, 82–83

reporting information, relationship between assessment, grading and, 7–8

resubmissions, 32–33

S

scale-based policies, 103–105

schools, readiness for grading reform, 132–134

Schroeder, M., 124

scores

    cut, 53–54, 83

    use of term, 6

    using, to reflect achievement levels, 50–54

scoring procedures, defined, 6

scoring rubrics, 51–54

self-determination, 25–26

self-efficacy, 26

self-reflection, 14

self-regulation, 26, 28–33

Spokane Public Schools

    Adams Elementary School, 30, 137

    Everett Public Schools, 66, 71–73, 106–110, 114–115, 116–119

learning-focused grading, development of, 137–141

standards

    curriculum versus state, 20–22

    grade on, 73, 75

    performance and content, 18–20

standards-based report cards, 23–24, 65–73

Stiggins, R., 28, 124, 138

student assessment, 7–8

students with special needs, standards-based grading for, 34–36

summative assessments, defined, 7

Swan, G., 36

T

teachers, readiness for grading reform, 127–131

Teachers of English to Speakers of Other Languages, 20

test items, writing good, 45–50

tests, preparing students for, 57–58

true/false items, writing, 46

V

validity

    communication, 120

    defined, 6

W

Weber, M., 30, 137–141

Well-Chosen Words (Power and Chandler), 121

Welsh, M., 16

Wiggins, G., 105, 136

writing good test items, 45–50

Embedded Formative Assessment

Dylan Wiliam

Emphasizing the instructional side of formative assessment, this book explores in-depth the use of classroom questioning, learning intentions and success criteria, feedback, collaborative and cooperative learning, and self-regulated learning to engineer effective learning environments for students.
BKF418

Formative Assessment & Standards-Based Grading

Robert J. Marzano

Learn everything you need to know to implement an integrated system of assessment and grading. Dr. Marzano explains how to design, interpret, and systematically use three different types of formative assessments and how to track student progress and assign meaningful grades.
BKL003

The Teacher as Assessment Leader

Edited by Thomas R. Guskey

Meaningful examples, expert research, and real-life experiences illustrate the capacity and responsibility every educator has to ignite positive change. Packed with practical strategies for designing, analyzing, and using assessments, this book shows how to turn best practices into usable solutions.
BKF345

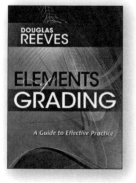

Elements of Grading

Douglas Reeves

Learn several strategies for improving grading practices, while examining the common arguments against reform. With this practical guide, you can improve grading to meet four essential criteria—accuracy, fairness, specificity, timeliness—and also make the process quicker and more efficient.
BKF410

Solution Tree | Press

a division of
Solution Tree

Visit solution-tree.com or call 800.733.6786 to order.